CHIPOLAR

CHIPOLAR

LIONEL HICKENBOTTOM
"El Antron"

CHIPOLAR

By: Lionel Hickenbottom aka El Antron

For Information about special discounts for bulk purchases please contact El Antron LLC Special Sales at elantron@elantron.org

Printed in the USA

Cover Art by El Antron
Print-ISBN: 978-1-7375543-0-1
eBook-ISBN: 978-1-7375543-1-8
El Antron LLC
PO Box 1022
Red Oak, Ga 30272
elantron@elantron.org
www.elantron.org

TABLE OF CONTENT

INTRODUCTION

The picture that I painted while coming up with this master piece was something that I envisioned.

It is possible that we can have the same tools and equipment and build something totally different. The main thing is starting something.

But not only starting something finishing what you started. Speaking life over what you create, see yourself doing great things.

You must go within, in order to discover what you are looking for, what you are searching for is your higher self.

I send good energy and hope that this body of work inspires you to start living in your higher purpose......Much Love!

CHAPTER 1

CHILDHOOD

Where you from? Southside, Southside. Where you from, Southside, uhh-oooh, uhh-oooh. To begin with, anybody that's familiar with St. Bernard hospital on the South Side of Chicago already knows the sense of urgency they have towards their patients, and this where I was born on April 5th, 1982. Just being taken at this hospital alone is where being Chipolar all begun, on everythang.

67th and Rhodes can't remember the exact address, but yea, that's the block I grew up on. Pops got us up out of there in 1985. Now that I'm understanding life, I get it now. Most Chicago people jokingly will throw a shot at you, like "naw you ain't from the city, fam you from the burbs, you a suburbanite." It's just like anyone else who comes from poverty comes across some money, and they are moving on up, like the Jefferson's. Back in the day, if you were Indigenous and lived in the South Suburbs or anywhere besides the inner city, you were "quote on quote," on another level.

To me personally, honestly, you were just experiencing less low frequency vibes, but the vibes you felt was on a whole different level and vice versa, then yo people in the inner city. So that analogy, if you lived in the burbs, and you had it made was cap. In addition, everyone that made this move back in this time still operated through the inner city of Chicago. My granny lived on 67th and Aberdeen, Auntie 71st and Chapel. I got family all through Englewood, and I'm plugged. I'm Chuckling just thinking about this. Living in the burbs, you got asked that question, "where yo girlfriend live?" Your Response, "My girlfriend lives in the city," that single answer got yo ass roasted every time, even if you did have you a weekend or summer girlfriend, when you went to the hood, but wasn't nobody going for that. At the same time, you show some type of fate that you had ties to the city at least on the weekend with your family, oh yeah, and church, so you weren't just no straight suburbanite.

This also is a development of Chi-polar, anyone will tell you this. Man, city boys use to prey on the suburbanites. They used to feel like it was a sweet lick. It's like they knew if you weren't interacting with the hood. It's like an oxymoron being Chi-Polar, because you had city boys that weren't going to the Burbs. Obviously, it was a Hate/Love relationship between City and Suburbanites while growing up in the late 80's all the way to like 1999, 2000. 20 yrs. later, and nobody wants to live in the south suburbs! Although for some, its still a safe haven. I'm just saying the south suburbs has always been a mini city. Don't forget we are some of the first towns outside of the city. Southside relatively speaking. As Maywood and Bellwood IL is to the Westside or out West. When my parents moved to Dolton in 1985, we were a raisin in the rice bowl. I stayed right across the street from Thornridge High school, right there on 149th and Sibley. Diversity played a significant role on me in society. Some of my best friends were Filipinos, the Renos. If you from the land, you know exactly who I'm talking about. Them was my brothers from another mother, Chuck, and Dan. Rodriguez and 'Jesus were my Latino hermanos, plus my Indigenous bros Ben and Ron Ron. My experiences as a shorty were expanding with the mixture of weekends and some summers on 67th and Aberdeen, or my ole man pushing his 1985 Lincoln and me riding shotgun on the way to one of his partners cribs in the projects, the Robert Taylor homes. My pops, everyone called him Hick. My ole man was smooth, and the man was smart if you look at it. Move to the burbs but be moving throughout the city as if you still live there. Typical shit people do now. Reason? Being like the Jefferson's, you are moving on up. So now you a Suburbanite and a City slickster.

CHAPTER 2

NEIGHBORHOOD

The Shit is just crazy as these memories began to surface in my membrane. Got chills going through my body just thinking about it. I remember getting introduced to sports! I did the music thing when I was young because my Auntie, Uncle, and Mom used to sing in the church choir. Took piano lessons and voice lessons at the age of 7. If I had known what I had known now, I would have stuck with music and never played sports. It's more longevity in the music game, in my honest opinion, and more money, too. If you aint trying to be a superstar, you can always stay independent and still eat. It's like I remember like it was yesterday; my mom's getting a call from my aunt on my dad side about signing up with the local tee ball at Dolton Boys baseball.

Unfortunately, this is when having rhythm, knowing C sharp, and me singing from the stomach, stopped for me. Back and forth from the burbs to the city, enrolled at Avalon

Park on 83rd, where I played Biddy League. We won a Championship and everything. My cousin Jimmy was the man. We were shorties he was putting up like 10 or 15. I bout had a couple of points, like 2 or 4. That was a lot for 7 yrs old, my cousin was hooping, though. Dell my uncle used to load up the van, and we used to be like ten deep coming from the burbs to go hoop at Avalon Park. The first year my parents signed me up for the Dolton Bears. We are talking like 1989, 1990, that 1st year we had a squad. We went 10-0, and our Varsity went 9-1. They lost one game to the New Lennox Mustangs. The score was 2-0. Fam, I remember it like it was yesterday. They were playing under the lights, pouring rain and muddy as fuck. Tee-Rae takes one to the house as he's running down the sidelines, the whole squad is throwing up the #1 sign, a 90-yard touchdown run, they call it back, they were sick. Early in the game in was tough as New Lennox held them for a safety. 2 to 0 crazy way to lose a game. Coaches knew talent, and they pulled it out of me. I played running back along with a couple of other guys, and I stood out. I was willing to compete. True story, I was coached by a guy named Coach Murloft. The most intriguing thing about Coach Murloft is that he was an ex-war veteran, and he coached us on one leg. Yes, he had one leg. Hats off to him from day one; he instilled something in me that I carry for life. And that is "no excuses, get it done."

Every Friday, right when practice would end, he would put us in a circle. He would put two guys in the middle with boxing gloves, and we would slug it out with full- bodied equipment. Maybe that played a part in my Chi-polar now that I think about it. You have two seven-year-old children running Oklahoma drills, and every Friday, they enter the ring with boxing gloves throwing blows. It plays an impact on their brains early. It becomes normality, it's like riding a bike, when you bred to go to the NFL, intensive training, I bout could have gone to the MLB and NBA. I was an all-around athlete.

Once I began to get acclimated to the community through sports, my outside influence not only came from the weekends spent in the city, but this suburban life that was somewhat normal. I became a Senator, a Dirksen Senator. I don't want to toot my own horn and be like I was the man, but ok, put it like this. I was that little shorty that had something about me. I was one of them guys. I learned various ways how to move as a young man. My cousin John, Dell, and Jimmy were a tremendous influence in my life. My cousin Marco and I are 1st cousins we did almost everything together cause my mom, and my aunt Annie is sisters, so I would also include my cousin Marco. I had two older sisters but being involved with what boys did was the concrete foundation of me being one of the few real men left cut from that thorough cloth, that's extinct in today society. It's a misperception of what a gang supposes to be built upon, structured, and utilized for, and that is to serve good deeds and protect their community. A gang of many people forms a group or gang. How about arranging together to work on one accord. Everything is a gang if it's more than a certain number of people, no matter your involvement. If you have attachments, then you are a member. The question is, are you active or non-active, and within that organization, what are you guys' intentions? Every gang is not bad if you guys are focusing on growth, development, betterment, peace, love and everything else embedded in the teachings. For some odd reason, I was always ahead of my time, and was that child that hung around older people, I wanted all the game growing up. It's just how it is in Chicago; you grow up fast, but remember, I'm back and forth from Dolton to city. Ideally, living in unfortunate conditions might hinder you from reaching your full potential, and that's innerstood but still not an excuse. It's different in the Chicagoland area! True, but don't get me wrong. Back in the day, we had parents involved in the local community, and we had Grandparents being Grandparents, the village raised us. We were still jumping off the porch early in the 90's. In 1992 I jumped off the porch and started politick with the streets. I was like 9 or 10 playing sports, running the streets with the locals on whatever side of town you would catch me on from Dolton to Harvey, through Riverdale, South Holland, Calumet City, and sometime Lansing. See if you had a bike, you could move around anywhere you wanted to, but after a while, hopping in a vehicle with the homies a little older was risky, but driving at 12 years old was usual but even riskier. I knew a couple of people driving around that age. I got into my first car accident at 11. It's just how we were moving —this where now you're almost fully Chi-polar by the age of 12. Furthermore, in my life, I have had good and bad influences! A part of my growth as a young man was my teacher, Mr. Scott/Coach for basketball. Besides my Pops and my uncles conducting yourself as a gentleman was something instilled in my generation, mixed with some Gangster stuff, this is what classified us as solid or well balanced. We had sense back in the day. We held the door for the ladies, even gave up seats for women to sit, more importantly we watched our mouths around elders, etc. Nowadays, all morals have been thrown out the window. Conscienceless, you would argue if you witnessed some of the things that we witness with disrespect from the younger generation. What? Growing up Yea, right, disrespecting; man, anybody liable to pop you in your mouth, cause your mother gave them the consent. The village was raising the village. So, carrying myself as a young man was something modeled by stand-up guys. By this time, I was full-time into whatever, though. When you are young and are exposed to worldly things, your mind begins to shape itself for its course in life. If I explained or told you every single detail what I did in my life or when I did it, you would innerstand, damn, Chi-polar is not a disease; it's a mental state, a survival tactic, the ultimate way to be one with yourself. By 7th Grade, I was fully in tune, and I started smelling myself. I thought my own shit didn't stank. Summertime usually consists of me leaving home at 9 am and sometimes not returning until nighttime, if not the next day or two. It was just too much to get involved in, especially being in the streets all day. I had been getting recruited at this time by some of the local members of organizations throughout communities to become a part of their movements. Facts, almost everyone who grows up in a specific neighborhood usually join forces with those in that area or you're stereotyped as being one of them.

For example, if you grow up around GD's nine times out of ten, you would be one. If your hood is manifested with Black peace Stones, you might just turn out one of the brothers. Vice Lords, Latin Kings, Four-corner hustlers, Black Gangster, BD to becoming a dealer or a killer. If it's habitual, you could turn out one of the other and be a whole star playing some type of sport. You know how many people gangbangers that was some of the most talented athletes who played sports. I'm talking real life potential. Even if you aren't gangbanging, Chicago was infested with gangs from day one. Long story short, and he wasn't even a Gang Member but watch the movie Cooley high. They killed Cochise and Preach found him dead. So, although you have the good examples being modeled through sports, some behaviors are modeled throughout everyday living cause most of the time, most are living in a struggle unmeaningly. So certain behaviors become normal, granted it might be wrong as all outdoors, but when you Chi-Polar, everything is right cause that's what you're taught to believe. My influences came from all walks of life. Imagine being molded by your parents, the streets, preachers, teachers, coaches, killers, dealers and respectfully can't forget about the members.

CHAPTER 3

COMMUNITY

Conversing with an individual not too long ago from Cali, I explained to him that back in the '90s, Chicago had just as many murderers versus some of the years in the 2000s. I wasn't praising it or anything, and it just shows nothing changed. As a shorty in Chicago, no matter what side you rode with, you were given some type of lit to live by that consisted of laws and policies to know how to conduct yourself. As an outstanding member, if you were active, you just couldn't move no any type of way. I could blame it on the older homies for steering me down some dark roads. In any situation, there is light if the bogus part is shun upon. I was always that one that was learning, getting all the knowledge and wisdom I needed to navigate through many paths in my life. Let me tell you, this way before my path even got lit. By eleven, twelve years of age, imagine being plugged in, all ya homies a couple of years older than you, and they driving you everywhere throughout the land.

Moreover, a gallon of gas was .99 cents. Throw $5 dollars in the tank, and we were on the go. Them boys had dirt bikes, you could put $1 in your tank and hit the trails, everybody and they mama was at the trails behind White Castles in Dolton, where Menard's is now. That use to be a dirt bike trail, and the same way they are chasing bike boys down, the Dolton bike boys use to give Robocop, Lacy, and them a run for their money. We were just a different breed coming up. Cuzo, fourteen, got his mama car all the time. It was so small, my homie Lil Phil use to call it Mr. Bucket, and he had the nerve to start singing the song "ah Mr. Bucket of fun, ah, Mr. Bucket use to get us everywhere. I was twelve years of age, and I was getting a little high by this time. Hold on, hold on, I'm going to let you know how the whole smoking thing started; I told you I hopped off the porch early. On this day of my accident, I told you all when I was like 11 or 12, and the homie Ben and I had blew a blunt. He always used to get his mama car; anybody that grew up in Dolton back in the '90s knows what I'm talking about. We were driving super young. Admirably, he comes out, we hop in the car, and we were gone, we all through Dolton, Riverdale, by the time we get to Calumet City, my homie extends me the opportunity to get behind the wheel. Did I? Fucking right, I did! My cousin John or Dell wasn't extending me that type of opportunity on their watch, but I always took notes. Ben "you wanna drive?" Me "Heck yeah," we switched seats. It was like Jesus took the wheel; I was driving like everyone else was, and it was my first time behind the wheel. Seat scooted up all the way like I'm a part of the little people community. My chest was smacked on the steering. Hit the block, we right there behind Nicky's Gyro, the street by the eway, back road. Like an experienced teenager, I was driving driving, next the street curves to the right to keep going straight along the way. I did not know how to maneuver the wheel and ride the curb swiftly. Another car was coming, and boom, I hit the car. Yea, man, damn, we pulled a hit and run. Police called the crib like three that morning, my momma swears it wasn't me. Shit, I did too. But the homie tricked on me, he confessed to his mother about the new 95 Camry I had damaged, including the other person's cars. I went to court, but for some odd reason, the judge dropped everything. I was back out here on my Dyno GT.

You can take the Indigenous person out the hood, but you can't take the hood out of the indigenous person, an infamous quote that sometimes proves one's right. The reason I'm saying that because by 96, the South Suburbs had problematic situations pertaining to gang wars, robberies, and killings. It wasn't just Pleasantville. As time went on and more and more people began to migrate to the South Suburbs, more and more destructive behavior was brought out. I will continue to embark on this. Almost everyone I knew could have played a major league sport; it was just that much talent in the South Suburbs. But I can admit the suburbs had the aspect of the streets as well, respectfully I can say. Most people there were from the inner city. 8th Grade, I was fully active, playing sports, even had a little size on me, wasn't the most handsomeness, but was popular enough to make something shake. I was gamed; you wouldn't believe half of the things I seen and done between the age of 9-11. Most events I still see vividly because it was a part of the mold, my character. Coming from an OG standpoint, seeing a child out here begging for change stirs my soul, the hustle in my soul. Making some money, for some reason, was always on my radar. I wanted things. Let it have snow, you would think I had my own lawn care service company. I would be all through the hood knocking on doors, shoveling driveways, raking leaves, running to the store for my favorite lady on the block. My favorite lady, whose name I will keep confidential, turned me on to a lot at a young age, 13. El, graduating from 8th Grade was a significant accomplishment. Looking back, they been implemented the program; no child left behind. I know I tried to comprehend the schoolwork, but I was enthusiastically gravitating to the outside influences. Although I was young, our generation, the eighty's baby tactics of surviving at that age became a task. I never had the desire just to be a super knucklehead, being strategic to avoid deep trouble and transitioning into a sophisticated leader was instilled from multiple sources. They said take some of the good and leave the bad, when trying to grasp what Chi-polar consists of, here is a simplistic way to understand this behavior; it's the bad and good being balanced in a way that keeps you grounded to sustain any circumstance and personally turn it into your righteous endeavor. Something to think about, that's some Chi-polar shit, right? Let them tell it, I was not that bright. Who would of ever thunk it? My divine light was illuminating everywhere I went unconsciously.

An ultralight beam, my light has always been lit, I'm talking about, beaming beaming. When pagers (beepers) first came out,

I had one of them joints. Benny and I, a different Ben, not the Benny I mentioned when I was in the car accident. Benny was my best friend from 1st Grade up until 8th Grade. Vividly, I remember bro and I walking home, were in Dolton. Man 2 BPSN members, they like in high School, see me playing with my beeper, I see them looking, I tried to be slick and put it in my draws, next thing you know, they like let me see that pager shorty? What do i do? Reach in my draws and gave it to them, with no regard of my sweating private parts directly touching the pager they still pimped off, I was sick. At that time didn't to many shorties have no pagers. I'm like in 3rd, or 4th Grade might have been 5th or 6th Grade. They were grown, though, I had seen one of them later in life and wanted to smack the shit out of em. That would lead to an all-out war. Besides learning upon my journey as a warrior, that stunt they pulled was super weak. I was super young. Relatively to the effect of why I became Chi-polar, here it is 25 plus years later, and it still replays in my head, because I would never let that happen again. Yup, safe to say by this time, I was on good bullshit. Experience after experience bottled up.

That summer leading into Freshman year, I had made a couple of opposition. For some reason, they wanted to test my Gangsterism. One of my brothers to this day banged to the left, a four- corner hustler; they were just different. No disrespect. That's the crazy thing in Chicago, people know the energies, the look, the way you carry yourself if you are one of the folks or one of the brothers, I might have discussed this early in the beginning.

CHAPTER 4

LOST BOY

Thornridge High School, I didn't have a chance. It's surreal now, the whole inner Dolton attended this School. I was remembering the epic summer that consisted of my character being recognized as an all-around ball of light. I had some of those enemies during gym class, if you are wondering how, I got an F during Gym class. Only thing I was trying to pass was a 28 sweep that was designed to throw to the open wide receiver down the field. Freshman year, I was the starting tailback. We had a squad out of this world. Most of my teammates I played along with were from Dolton Bears, few players, no coaches. Effortlessly we went 0-9 as a freshman year football team. Now, where did we go wrong? I have the slightest idea. Flashback playing against the Bradley Boilermakers, I had like eight touchdowns; they called 6 of them back. I was out there juking they ass, taking it straight to the house, touchdown. You already know! By the end of the game, I was whooping some ass on the field, and someone off my squad was pulling me up off some random white boy. Whenever I run into my homie Monroe, that's what he talks about, like "El, you remember you were punching the shit out of that white boy during the game?" I am like, on everything I love, I don't remember. That's that Chi-polar, cause knowing me, I was on some bullshit, they were cheating us. I could say they were racist, but honestly, growing up, we saw no colors, now, if someone was an asshole, that was that. Is it safe to say history was hidden in some demographics? Versus the Deep South and other places which experience racism? South Suburbs had segregation, but who would of thunk it? Dolton was intermingled. By my second semester, I found myself running through the courtyard with a couple of the guys, scrapping an opposition. I think whoever introduced the world killa at the end of whatever, they are an evil genius, allowing those who uses it to ignite an instant fire to one's fuel. Just say woowopdabamskip killa, whoever woowopdambamskip is, will be looking for you for the disrespect you put on that name. It still happens to this day—something something, killa. Regarding tuning up a couple of punks up in the schoolyard, not only did I have the school security guard called Easy-E on me. I had the law on me, my dean, and the oops, trying to find a way to punish me. My name's ringing throughout the hood, they started labeling me a gang leader. I Disappeared like a thief in the night, never showed back up to Thornridge high school again; I was now a dropout.

One morning I got caught by my favorite lady on the block walking the opposite way from school. I stayed right across the street literally, come out of my house, walk across the street and to the right. I'm going down cottage grove towards the store, Fairway. She comes out of her house, "where are you going?" Me, "Ummm, meet my friend!" It was just a normal conversation without having any suspicious of me, ducking, dodging, and ditching school because I was the cause of a big gang fight. She ain't play that shit and thought I was very intellectually inclined to indulge in her low-key street business. Already having a run-in with some more unmotivated older guys who thought they needed to snatch my weed when I was 12 years old. I had got my first pack from one of the older guys, which was my homie brother I used to hoop with all the time. Big bro started me off with— $ 100 pack of some good regular reefer. I'm riding on my bike, see them walking, tell them I got weed, they ask for four bags and ran off faster than Jessie Owens at a track meet. It was no way I was catching these overgrown guys, although I was athletic, my muscle development hadn't kicked all the way in beginning of my teen years. I proceeded to get my serve on, but I was short on the pack money. My Favorite lady found out about my situation and covered the difference. This was after I told big bro I was short cause some older Solid Four corner hustlas who knew not to fuck with him had snatched my pack. He wasn't trying to hear any of that, so I had to come up with that money. Watching every move, I made from here on out, moving a pack meant guarding it with my life. I was destined not to be a failure at this point. I had already stopped going to school by this time. It was going on about three weeks, I was failing every class, but I was getting that cash. As my cousin would jokingly say, "you care about your looks more than your books." A couple of errands here and there for my favorite lady became quite lucrative, besides during the day, I would hang out at her house once she found out I dropped out. I was classified as straight flunky, at this point for myself dropping out of school and me being her flunking. The little money I was making, I was bringing in grocery at home, parents still thinking I'm just petty hustling cause at that age, I kept a few hundred dollars in my pocket. Unfortunately, things became obvious once my report card came home. A 0.095, I told you I even failed Gym, I think I got some points in lunch. Straight up. My mother saw my report card and was speechless. For some odd reason, she ain't even trip. She didn't tell my pops, and that's for sure. It would have been a problem. "Lionel, what are you going to do, and what have you been doing?" My mom asked? I told her I had a situation that went on, and I didn't think it was safe to go back and left it at that. My mother was innerstanding she knew what type of young man I was, I never brought a problem home, far as police or bogus run in, in the streets. Stories, later on, gave her a perception of what I was doing in my early teen years.

I had to figure it out, and I had to figure it out quickly. I had built tough skin through some experiences early on that made me equip for a struggle. It began to get rough, chance after chance, errand after errand, money was good, but I learned I had made some enemies that weren't appeased by my transition. I learned I was a target while hanging on

143rd, and Drexel and the Slick boys rolled up, they ran my name, and what came to my attention they had labeled me a leader of the Gangster Disciples. If they had said Leader of Growth and Development, it probably would have been believable. I'm all about righteousness. Wrong is wrong, right is right. I begin to see things go left. It was time to get little.

CHAPTER 5

INFLUENCES

Fortunately, I moved around, everything just started to go right. One thing I will say, a true Chicagoan can correct me if I'm wrong, we had some praying Grandma's! I was a faithful member for a very long time at Green Grove Missionary Baptist Church, growing up right there on 67th and Marquette. Don't Let my OG drop us off at my Grandma crib for about two weeks. Yea, ok, we were in church Sunday, Wednesday, damn near Friday, and for sure Saturday. All Programs, Christmas speeches, the books of the Bible songs, all that good stuff is instilled in a person who is Chi-Polar. Hit you with a "Lord please rebuked the devil, in a minute. GOD usually sends the right Angels to come to guide you through adversary.

Never in a million years did I ever think I would be enrolling at Paul Robeson High School. Going home to the south suburbs., my mom would make that right on 67th Marquette, make another right on 67th Morgan, then make that left on 69th. I rode past Robeson often, 69th and Normal, it was insane. I had an older cousin; she was plugged in, First Lady of the S.O.S at the time. She went to the Robe, and I remember my mom's receiving a phone call about her being kidnapped after school in the parking lot. Riding past it to get on the expressway was the only time I ever really seen myself in front of it. It dawned on me one morning, I had dropped out of high school. The image of what I was portrayed as, coincided with the perception of what you think going to high school in the heart of Englewood is perceived to be like. Picture lean on me. Would it be safe to say for all my Raiders at that time, Coach C was Mr. Clark. The cool Mr. Clark, though, Coach C.

Retrospectively, how I manage to lean towards Robeson, respectively a legend went there that played for Dolton Bears, my bro bro, Squeak. Squeak, old man, was the reason behind the evolution of my life. Going to Robeson High School was one of the greatest things that happened to me. I will explain more later in this chapter. Hootie, he, and I became close past summer through a couple of interactions in the streets and playing baseball. My ace boon, Hootie is the friend every friend could ask for, he is the definition of loyalty. Knowingly the same story as most suburban living shorties, they moved from the city. Fool had got kicked out of Thornridge, pretty much for the same demonstration, having to put the hands on someone. He one person you don't want get to get socked by. Bro ended up going to Robeson. Growing up playing Dolton Bears, we often surrounded ourselves with a dedicated players who participated every year. Lil' Stan played on my Dolton Bears team, in my first year, we went 10-0. Living on 136th, bro was in between the border of Riverdale and Chicago. I learned later Lil' Stan also was attending Robeson at the time. One of the first times my light bulb clicked on that I could feel the electric pulse radiating from toe to head. On this particular morning, I had a suggestion that led to my growth and development into a conducive teenager and not just some hoodlum. "Ma, I could go to Robeson, Squeak go there, Hootie; you remember Lil Stan played Widgets with me on Dolton Bears?" My mother replies, "for real?" The most mind-boggling part of this suggestion, I didn't even know Robeson high school was the same School I rode past frequently. Granny stayed on 67th and Aberdeen. Consciously, I just never paid attention and thought, this would be my next righteous endeavor. Granny staying on 67th and Aberdeen made it that much easier for me to enroll. My mama got on it as soon as possible. I don't even think she thought it in a million years I would be going to Robeson the Old Parker High School.

She was also a graduate of Parker High School. You often heard stories about the kid in the class that lived in the city that went to a suburban school. This story was the opposite for four young men. We were traveling every day from the suburbs to the city. My mom was working out west at the time, but she had linked up with Squeak's father, Mr. P, to see if I could hitch a ride every day to school. At this time, Mr. P, who I will call P, was already picking up Hootie every morning, then he would swing by Lil' Stan's house to get him, had welcomed me in with open arms. Every morning my mother would wake me up and drop me off at Hootie's house.

Bebeeeeeeep beep, beep, beep bebeeep, the sound of a loud 1992 Mercedes Benz 500, there to alert us, 6:15 am, let's go. I wasn't going to impede on this routine and adjusted quickly. Once he scooped us, Hootie and I, he would then hit the back road and grab Lil Stan. Beebeeeeep beep be beep beep. As soon as we hit the block, that's all you would hear, and we not even in front of the house yet, man, you better be ready to go, Mr. P wasn't playing. There weren't too many fathers out there that stepped up to teach other children, if it wasn't their own. I mean, you must take your hats off to these types of men in the communities. Here it is; he made it his preference to get up every Am and made sure we got to school on time. Mr. P also made sure we rode in style. It was like a dream, catching up on Z's on the way to school, when I woke up, it felt like I was in a different world. If you could hear the music playing in my head just envisioning myself hopping out that Mercedes Benz 500 class on the first day of school on 69th and Normal, in the heart of Englewood.

Guns and Roses song, "Welcome to the Jungle." Imagine the movie "Lean on me." Let's nip this in the bud, Chicago's well known Mr. Larry Hoover went to Parker high school, which later became Paul Robeson High School, facts. It was a whole different vibe than going to Thornridge. Out there in the burbs, where I was super tough. I wasn't scared or nothing, fam, I just fell right in line. It was my first day of school, not theirs. "Ooooooh, Squeak, what up?" "Hey Hootie," Lil Stan;

greeted with love, I witnessed the good off rip. Breakfast was essential, I learned as we were there faithfully, them Super doughnuts heated up, was fire. It was the ultimate way to kick off your day full of adventure. Wow, just thinking about it, the programming of the educational system is hypnotic. Educational institutions are bogus for teaching us them lies to indoctrinate us, and if you don't learn it, you fail. On my first day in school, I realize I was now challenged to fail and pass at the same time. I wasn't the smartest person in the world, but I knew if I failed any challenge, I wouldn't pass the ultimate test of being bout that life. I Midas. Yea, I Midas, I had to look up the definition of Midas, which means everything he touched turned into gold. I had no problem plugging in with some of the guys, a couple of young tenders, and I was good. Nothing suburban was about me, we were all the same. Ready for defense if it means your life.

CHAPTER 6

DEMO

I quickly adapted to the environment. Grades wise I was supposed to be a sophomore, but I was a demo. In other words, a flunky. But by my second semester, I was caught up and was now in my right Grade. Football season had come around, it was now time for tryouts. The varsity had been working out all summer, getting ready for the upcoming season. I thought I was about to go straight to varsity. Coach C was the varsity football coach at Robeson for the past 20 years. I didn't get quite introduced to the coach yet, boy, when we did meet, the greet, was not welcoming. Announcements sounded throughout the early AM after the pledge of allegiance, "Today is football tryouts," the Secretary says. Either she just said that, or I was tweaking cause when I went out for tryouts, it was for freshmen and sophomores. After School, I reported to the varsity football field as if I would join the roster right then and there. "Hey, what's up, Coach?" I'm Lionel, I'm here to try out, I said. "Coach C," he responded. Coach then proceeded to explain to me that it was not tryouts for varsity because the guys had worked so hard during the summer it wouldn't be fair for me to join the team right there. I went straight to the freshman and sophomore tryouts. Talent speaks for itself. I was out there performing. There was no way I was getting cut from the squad. Roughly about 5 minutes into the tryouts, Coach C came over there snapping on me. All you hear is, "motherfucker didn't I tell you, son, you couldn't try out, this is freshman and sophomore's son you to old." I probably was 14 or 15 at the time. I told him my age and grade status, and he walked off scratching his head only to witness an all-purpose athlete. By the end of the season, the playoffs, I was starting cornerback against Mather, Harper, and Dunbar High School on the varsity level. That was the year Dunbar had Russell, he was nice. Squeaky and Russell were the 2 top athletes, along with a lot of other respected football players in CPS.

My first year as a Raider was astounding. I hoop too. All my teammates had attended either Bills or Nicholson Elementary School. I was the only outcast on the squad, so I had to prove myself that I was a hooper and also one of the guys. Respectfully, I never had a problem putting up no buckets. In games, I would put up a quiet ten points, might give you fifteen. The chemistry amongst the team sometimes felt unbalanced because I went to school in the suburbs. My game was different, and they had all pretty much grew up playing together. Coach D at the time, saw something in me. I wasn't going. Buttons often get pushed. That's funny; one day, we on our way to a game, I rarely interact with too many cats on the team. I was always on some quiet shit. One day, I was sitting in front of the bus, we on our way to play Crane High School.

Reminiscing, I feel something clonk me in the back of my head with a couple of giggles. My Chipolar instantly kicked in simultaneously. I zoomed in on the first person that looked creeped out and gave him a two-piece spicy with mild sauce. They thought I lost it, foofop bop was all you heard. Coach D had no idea what happened. I think that game I started. From there, I never had a problem with fam again. I was a problem on the court, I had handles. I could see the court; I had a shot. I grew up playing with a lot of South Suburb Legends and got coached by some of the best. I took that game to the city and learned city ball. Facts, Janeiro Pargo, went to Robeson, and I beat him one on one. We were playing up to five, I beat him four to five. He swore up and down, Coach Red demand he loose that game on purpose, cap. I just can't believe, Coach Red told him to let me win. I don't think y'all know how hard I work for that last point. Janeiro Pargo, in High School, was a God on the court and a legend. But I can't wait to run into bro and see if he still going to stick with that same script. I was an all-around athlete. I even played baseball in High School.

I was walking righteous often hooking up with the wrong person, it was like a movie. I was pulling up to school as always, hopping out of the car approached by Big House, a senior who played football. Big house flashes two blunts and says, "I got two blunts," imagine that. Lil Stan wasn't there that day, squeak rejected the quick smoke session, Hootie and I joined in. We parked on 70th and Eggleston and hot box in a 1987 cavalier. This is 7 am. I was high as a kite. As we head into school, the energy and vibe were off. Instantly getting pushed to the left as we come in, and with no metal detectives, they had a random CPS raid. Oh no. They were locking up people if they had a pair of scissors not caring if you a had 3rd period art class. I had just blown two fat ass blunts and instantly wasn't high, they blew it quick. I didn't know what to expect, at this time, I had a beeper on me. I tell House, "man G, I have a pager on me." He replied, "just give it to the officer if you turn it in, they won't arrest you because you turned it in. I made it to easy for them, it was a layup. " All you hear is come with me sir, they took me to a room where they stretched me and dispersed everything out of my bag. I had already given them my beeper, they seen my baseball uniform. "Oh, you play baseball?" the officer asked. By this time Coach C and my baseball Coach came into the room, Coach C just shook his head. Anyone that smoked weed and he found out, he would refer to you as smoking that shit. He would always say, "you smoking that shit" made you feel like you were a hype, a clucker. They hauled me off to jail for having a beeper. I was sitting in jail high as giraffe's pussy. My mother came and got me after sitting for about 8 hours. We had a raw ass team in baseball.

CHAPTER 7

POPULARITY

My sophomore year, I played varsity. It was tough playing some teams. If anyone knows Chicago knows there are boundaries throughout the city. Your school represents what type of gang affiliation you are tied to. Just imagine the Folks playing the Moes (Blackstones). Let's say Robeson versus Tilden High School. 47th and Union, nothing but Stones. We hit a homerun some of our players doing the folks handshake on the field. They are doing the short cut Black Stone handshake, grip, drops the rakes, come back up, slap the 5, beat their chests. We both being disrespectful. Here it is we are playing a high school baseball game. We got to running up the score, them boys put in a phone call for a little aid assist. This was about to become bigger than baseball. The last inning was going kind of long, too long, enough time for the rest of the Moes to come up to the park. I guess Coach Rob had got a whiff of the hoodlums, he reached in his fanny pack, a chrome 380. I wonder if that joint would at least make some kind of noise.

You don't put that little motherfucker away in my Harlem night's voice. We made it out of there safe, I can say though. After losing to Hubbard high school in the first Inning 13 to 0 was devastating, they were smacking my homie Gino shit all over the park. Their pitcher pitched a no-hitter. Our season didn't last that long, a couple of us was declared ineligible, the team fell apart, wasn't many of us to begin with. I think it was 13 of us; you need 11 to play. Robeson was always known for having a small team. Our football team we only had 18 players. It was some beautiful woman in High School, I was trying to score with a couple of them. Especially since sports activity had slowed down. After School now consist of exploring what the South Side of Chicago Englewood streets had to offer. I had got acquainted with some solid individuals, we would link up and hit the block. I rotated back and forth between my grandmother's house and the burbs. Spending the majority of my time throughout the Englewood blocks allowed me to become official. When you from Chicago, it's just a certain way you got to move, that's when that Chipolar becomes a superpower. Who remembers the 16in bones rims? Squeak senior year copped a 1994 Celica with some 16in bones. I was a different type of teenager, my friends, too. It like we never had a curfew we always had freedom. Our Am on the way to school would now only consist of Lil Stan, Hootie, Squeak, and I. Stan got the swishers and the trees, we hit the store over the hill right there on 136th, if they wouldn't serve us any liquor, the shrimp boat on 130th would. Mama always told me, but papa never showed me, so I live my life as a thug, and all I wanna do is smoke weed, ride, and sell drugs,

Master P drowned out our ears through the speakers of a 1994 Celica sitting on 16 in bones flicking on the way to school. An early Am session was mandatory on the way to school, bumping that Ghetto Dope.

A lot was happening at that time, far as if I was bout it bout it, I was still low-key a problem. Hootie had play sister going to Curry High school on 49th And S. Archer. The difference in CPS vs Suburban schools is that Suburban schools have a homeroom period, which is the first period of the day. The teacher takes attendance, you skip any class after that, they just check with your homeroom teacher. CPS, you have division class, and that's at like 10 o'clock. Most of the time, that's when most people would leave school to partake in other festivities. It was even sweeter if you had a class in the old building, Parker high school. After division, Hootie rounded up a couple of the guys, and we hopped on the CTA headed to Currie. Almost every guy Hootie rounded up was suffering from Chipolar, including myself, on this day. We arrived Currie High school kind of early, and their next class period hadn't yet transitioned. Their school wasn't like ours or lean on me where they had chains on the doors. Slightly reminding me of Thornridge, there were no chains on any of their doors, designed somewhat similar. As we enter the building through a side-open door, we began to get spotted by students who recognized we didn't belong. They could smell trouble. Four dudes from Robeson with Chipolar marching through someone else high School, ready to put the hands on Hootie play sister victim. She had made a call to Hootie dad stressed that she had a problem with some guy.

It's been an ongoing problem, and she finally came up with a solution. Call Her play, brother. Luckily the guy had skipped class after division. He must have felt the vibes. He wasn't too in tune, we caught up with him later on that night and beat the brakes off him. Knock knock, is woowoodabam here, Hootie asked. We paid him a little visit and his girlfriend's parents' house. Her mom went to go get him, when he met us at the door, all you were hearing was "foofop, foo, bop, bop, bink ah bink." Her mother yelling historically, "stop." Things are different now, it could have easily gone the other way, and his moms could have blown one of our brains out. Honestly, I think she was more worried about us beating his brains in. Fighting back in the day, if you had one, some you would have to gladiate, and some was a one-hitter quitter. I had a confrontation in the hallway one day. I was giving one of my homies some aid and assist, someone told Hootie I was downstairs fighting. He never broke stride, "pow" one-hit would have him seeing little birds circle around his head as he slides down the nearest pole for support. Shit, happen so quickly the security guard we use to call "Big Killa" came and ask me why I do that boy like that? No punishment, I thought to myself, I'm plugged in. The next day in lunch, somebody sent the same boy off, and he wanted a rematch. I beat him to a pole, when he got up, the man's jaw was hanging like an almost broken tree limb. After doing this, I didn't feel good about myself. He got suspended, not me, see how Chipolar is developed. Crazy right, you get beat up and suspended. He probably Chipolar now, bet he is. I'm sending peace and love to his universe. I was active but not always involved. We all had our shed of fights. Things just happened randomly, but if it involves my people, we knew. I was sitting in class one day, and Hootie come storming into my class, "come on, G, Lil Stan fighting," we had got there but too late. Kejuan and he had a two-on-two fight against BD affiliates. Lil Stan was one of the only BDs at Robeson high school, which wasn't many. All four got suspended, and that's how I ended up running track that year.

CHAPTER 8

STREET RUNNER

The track team had only consisted of 6 people at that time and Lil Stan and Kejuan, were two of them. I was always quick, but not fast. I got threw in the fire quick. Remembering running my first track meet at Englewood High School. If you didn't know, I smoked and drank, you would have never known I did both, faithfully. Sad, I know, you thinking like, weren't you an athlete? Yea, but I was exposed to a lot. Don't get it twisted; I knew what to mess with and what not to mess with. Catching an instance Charlie horse, after the 4x200. I was hurting, first event was a breeze, though. 4 runners. Everyone running 100 meters. Hitting the curve like Hussain bolt, you would have thought I was a world-class track runner. The next event, 4x200, it was ugly, an extra 100 meters at a high speed, whoa. That first 100 meters, I had no knowledge of coming out the block at a certain speed to just enough to kick the second gear up and then finish strong. Coming out the blocks, it was full force, by the next 100 meters, look like I was being rewind, as the other runners were being fast forward. Eventually realizing my legs felt like spaghetti, we skipped the next event, the 4x400, in respect of my legs, they were dead. I was being real with myself; it was no way I was running around that track at full speed without throwing up my guts. I might have seen the upper room; I wasn't in tip-top shape and ready to compete for a title. If you never ran track in high school, unarguably, I will tell you it's one of the best sporting events to attend. It's like 30 gangs meet up to run it out. Guys and girls are competing. Almost every high school in the city there, it be jumping. The Year of 1998, Eastern Illinois University hosted the State track meet that year. They hosted the Women's a week before the Men. Arriving a day before the state track meets, we properly prepared to outrun whomever. That night they threw a party for all teams, but what's a party without a drink. Rounding up a couple of bucks and voted who would go get us the Remy Ma Vsop to get us out our body. Lil Stan would be the candidate. Later, we met up in the park before hitting the party, taking a couple of swigs of some cheap ass Willie P would put Lil Stan in the roasting chair. "You big ugly, man, you went and got some Wille P bro? We drunk some of the best growing up, Remy, Crown, Hennessy, don't get me wrong, we knew about Cisco, E&J, and Paul Mason. If we had a choice, top shelve were preferred. Going to the club, as usual, we danced with every female at the party. We didn't care if they were with their boyfriend, most them were locals, might have been some college girls, now that I'm thinking, at least freshmen. By the end of the night, a couple of cats had scored, I took one for the team. Still, until this day, Lil Stan going to see me, and if this comes about, all he is going to say is "Nene." I dropped the baton on that one. Good thing I was on reserve, the meet the next day had come Coach C and I prepared the guys for the first event. Warm-ups were intense, Squeak's first leg, Gerome second, Lil Stan third, Greg last leg. First event, 4x1, the sound of a 22-caliber gun is heard. "Pow" Squeak coming out the blocks was textbook as he gets a jump on every lane. Passing the baton to Gerome promptly perfected for a course on how to pass a baton in track. 1,2,3 reach, we were in the fastest heat, Gerome's technique sound as he receives the baton. I can see Coach C observing the stop clock watch and the perfection of greatness. 1,2,3, reach, the vibration and the energy dropped to the lowest Megahertz produced by the universe. The transaction between Lil Stan and Gerome somehow did not coincide in the same frequency, and Lil Stan dropped the baton. Wow, Robeson High School, on the way to set the state record for the fastest time ever in history, had just gone out the window in a split of a second. "Motherfucker" with a long country city accent, "He been smoking that shit." The look on my face astounded by what I had just witnessed, my reply, "naw Coach, he ain't smoke" I ain't lie, I ain't tell him we had a couple of drinks either. Bro wasn't a drinker though, I preferred him to smoke because he never tweaked like that, not even off weed. Truth is Coach C was sick, we were all sick. We both get roasted for dropping the baton when we were downstate.

Not everyone is an athlete. You got full-time athletes, full-time street dudes, part- time athletes and part-time street dudes, nine times out of ten the ones working part-time indulges in the streets sometimes but often play sports. Part-time athletes usually play sports but gravitate to the streets. I was full-time Athlete, and I would say form 1099 street guy. Walking down 65th and green and a 1987 Monte Carlo approaches the block slow. We were coming back from the store headed to Gregs house, where we hung out at kicking the bobos. To be aware is to be alive, cause if Lil Stan did not see his enemy, he saw from the two-on-two fight previously in the lunchroom, his revenge would have been sweet as it came. Greg was BD, Lil Stan was BD, they were BD, I was the only one, not a BD. BD or not, I don't think any of that mattered at the time. By the time they bust a U-Turn, Stan had taken off running. Track training had become beneficial. "Man, fam, you should take off too," Greg says. I was stuck in my tracks. If you ever got caught in the wrong person hood and felt defenseless, I feel your pain. They pulled up like the Chicago slick boys, throwing the car in park in the middle of the street. "Where your boy go, Greg?" He Asked. Lil, Stan was probably on 68th and something, depending on the route he took to the L station. Why didn't I run? I have no idea. "Ain't you, GD," he replied. "Fam, we ain't even on that," I said. I could have been BD, and although Stan was one of my best friends, it would have been BDs against BD because they didn't care about that at all. It's like GOD swiped his Angels in to come to save me, not saying I would have got whooped, but I was in their hood, and it was an open ball game. Besides, they knew it wouldn't have been that easy to put their hands on me. It takes at least 20 minutes to come from the wild wild 100's. After that fight, Lil Stan put a phone call into his big brothers, and they were up at Robeson in like 10 minutes. The bros pulled up with a couple of choppers on business ready to Swiss cheese whoever. They posted up in front of the school when school let out, Kejuan was still lingering around even though he was suspended. He had never met Stan's older brother but had a sensibility of who he was, as he approached the car where he recognized an unfamiliar face, the chopper got upped on him. "Naw naw now, I'm the one that was helping your brother," they ain't never met him and looked him as an opposition. As I was exiting the building just in time, I was able to introduce them two. Things would get conflicting, if they would have caught Lil Stan in the hood and did something to him, it wouldn't been a good look if they had put their hands on me, his bro would have let bullets ring out in any direction of the person who he thought was a part of his brother fight. A situation like that would make you Chipolar. That's how we rode out.

CHAPTER: 9

IN MOTION

That summer, my uncle Theo had a 1979 Malibu. Offering it to my cousin was his first option, but after getting a rejection, I hooped in it. Just turning 16 a 1979 Malibu, you couldn't tell me anything, getting to point A and point B was efficient to see what was popping anywhere I was invited. That following school year lil Stan and I traveled to school by ourselves. Hootie and Squeak were class of 98, so Mr. P had full filled his duties of volunteering as a good guy. Our AM's would now consist of just us two and a blunt in the ashtray. Stopping on 71st and state at the candy store faithfully in the Am was a ritual. Figuratively speaking as a ritual, it was something we did every morning. It was Lil Stan hustle, stock up on candy, sell it at school, and triple his money. This was a little safer cause we could have sold the nose candy and made a killing. We were living like men in some instances. After School, once practice was over, hitting the Englewood blocks would get us aquatinted more with our people. My grandmother had got admitted to the hospital after a couple of strokes that limited her mobility. Not only was it my duty to check on her every day, but her house also had to be accompanied, so no break-ins would occur. Instead of me traveling back and forth to Dolton, I decided to move into my grandmother's house. While I was coming up long down the line, I bump my head a couple of times. I wasn't ruthless, I was reckless, after getting in trouble a couple of times, I remember my mother saying it wasn't her battle. That was the day she put everything in GOD's hands. It was also the day I realize I had to pray and ask GOD for protection. I have been on my own with GOD leading the way since. "I ask GOD to protect you and guide you and cover you in the blood of Jesus" is the words muttered from my mother. The perfect soundtrack to my life at that moment, Donny Hathaway, "little ghetto boy." One day I had to face responsibilities. The hustler in me wouldn't let me go without, I could still hit up my favorite lady on the block and make a couple of drops off to keep some money in my pocket. Once Hootie and Squeak graduated, my homeboy Greg and Ty Ty filled in for the substitution.

Greg was a player, and Ty Ty was a Hustler Hustler. My fullback, which was Denny at the time, joined the forces, and we were now five deep. We were at the age we were all facing responsibilities, and our parents didn't put curfews on us. Our moms had all met on a couple of occasions, and once that relationship was established, I think they prayed collectively that we all would be on a righteous path, and we were out there. With my grandma in the nursing can you imagine a 16-year-old child living by himself with four of his friends coming and going? Lil Stan and I had limited ourselves going out to the Wild wild hundreds unless we were going to get more clothes or him seeing his grandmother. 67th Aberdeen would be our full-time stay without parent supervision, thank GOD I had the protection over me. Most 16-year-old children would be irresponsible, not this 16 years old.

Made it to school on time every day, even with an AM wake and bake. People speak down on gangs. From the knowledge I was given, a gang was organized to protect the community. A lot of literature is misconstrued cause people don't read. Knowledge, wisdom, and understanding are three powerful words, gang-related or life-related. Let's talk about social development, politics, economics, and unity. These are all vital to our communities' hoods have been infrastructures by the enemy. One thing I did as a young boy growing up was listen. I wanted to soak up all the game I could to survive in the streets and in life. On this particular day, we had just got out of football practice.

Normal routine after practice hit one of the blocks, and we were spending at least $40 on some good weed and blazing all night. Coming down 69th, I see the slick boys (Chicago undercover man) riding past, before we know it, they were hooking a U-turn headed straight for us. I made left on 67th and Aberdeen, saying what's up to someone I knew standing in front of OK's grocery store. As we emerging to park in front of my house, I see in the rearview mirror four slick boys looking like demons ready to attack. I'm known throughout the city for football, say my name, and it's like candy man. Future reference to my young indigenous kings, don't throw your car in park and hop out to aggress the aggressor.

Moreover, I was staring down the barrel of a Glock .45. "What the fuck you are getting out the car for" the cop says. Sounding like a local member of the opposite gang, he had me shook as if I was on the wrong block. "Officer, what's going on, we just came from football practice" he wasn't trying to hear none of that. We were suspect, riding four deep, just left the block where we just reup to touch the sky, over some good Mary Jane. Thank GOD I didn't reach, they would have blown my head off. Gracefully he ran my license seen my last name and told me to have a good day, and we better win Friday against Corless high school. I think with our moms praying for us, and we were delivered from hurt, harm, and danger. Growing up, I would be the first one to tell you, living in the suburbs doesn't mean you are rich or wealthy. There were many days and nights we had an intermediate family gathering and sent prayers up to GOD and ask him to send a paying Angel our way to help with the mortgage. Sometimes meals were limited at home. There were many times where I stood in a church line to receive that Government peanut butter, thick ass cheese, and those nasty fucking powder eggs. People get it misconstrued about suburbanites, early on in your life, your parents might have come across some money, but that didn't mean they had any. In high school, once my mother washed her hands on me, finding ways to eat became a skill. This skill not so hard to manage when you had the hook up at multiple fast-food joints. At this time, I was involved with a female in high school who worked at Wendy's. Many nights she fed me and my homies. How you get a hookup and so much food? If you got the hook up in the drive-thru, order some fries. That's just the underplay for the overplay. When approached at the window by the cashier, just smile and always talk in coded language. You never want to raise the eyebrows of the manager. Things had to go smooth, I had three other people with me that had to eat too. When receiving your fries, somehow magically, it appears to be a bag full of burgers and a bag full of fries. Most of the time, KFC was our first option, Ty Ty and I both had some seniors working the drive thru. KFC used to be a hit, a big bucket of chicken and some potato wedges. Imagine smoking ten blunts and afterward smashing out a big bucket of Original Recipe chicken. It wasn't no starving.

I know I broke some hearts back in the day. I was young dumb, and full of fun. Although it's not a relationship, I didn't regret. Inadvertently, some girls I would kick to the curb after the feelings were getting too deep. Who said being in love shit isn't real? Break the wrong person's heart, and they deeply in love with you, they will experience a heart aching pain. I thought I was a player. I started dealing with a female that was involved with one of my homie homies. He wasn't my homie. Many reading this and instantly categorize me as a doucebag. If anything, she was bogus and not me. At that time, her boyfriend was getting money, I was making my errands, but those runs weren't consistent. A couple hundred here and there for dropping off an ounce or two was good for a 16 year older. Her guy had a block though, wasn't any competing with that, he was raking in money from Sunup to Sundown. What can I say, he had a lot of time on his hands, especially since he wasn't enrolled in school, although we were the same age. Honestly, she was my school girlfriend because they lived together during the time. If she would have got caught with me red-handed outside of school, lord knows. Feelings began to get involved. Long talks on the phone in high school, y'all had to go together. It was many nights; conversations were brief if we spoke outside of school. Urging to hook up outside of school, I invited her to my house and made her feel at home. We got this saying after engaging with a new woman, and you scored. The question is, did you mildew or BBQ? I'm not the type of guy to lie on my, you know what! Now that I'm older and learned the art of sex, I mildewed. Every man can be a witness to this, but if you are too excited, you might not perform well. After dry humping for a long period, I had pre-ejaculated in my pants. Furthermore, it wasn't no telling when he was getting back up. My joint had used up all my blood flow. Still eager to penetrate her walls, my limpness wouldn't allow me to bust through. She still hopped on it. Can a woman get pregnant through pre-ejaculations? Many Children came through the birth canal of a courageous woman. A child also exited from a man that probably mildewed and didn't BBQ. It was always questioning if I had a child out of her floating in the world. I will touch more on that topic later in my college years.

CHAPTER 10

FITTING IN

My senior year, after losing the bumper of my 79 Malibu and the Muffler, my hoopty started to break down. I was still riding; I tacked a big piece of wood measured out to a T sliding right in place of the bumper fitting exactly like Tetris. The muffler gone; you would have thought I had some flow masters on that baby. Shit was super loud. You heard me coming a mile away. I hadn't made a run or two, or at least, I wasn't good with stacking my money. Besides some fresh as gear, fresh kicks, and a fire ass blunt of Reggie, I bout could have stacked till I couldn't have stacked it no more. Once the law towed my malibu from the corner of my parents' home. I couldn't go back to a Dyno Gt. It was a car auction going on at the time at the Dolton Expo center. Chilling at my cousin John's house one day and got a whiff the auction was selling a 1989 Cutlass, everybody, and their mama was trying to get it. I was short on a couple dollars. Checking in with mom dukes and ran it past her, she ran me the $500 hundred. I pulled up in

Dolton the next day on my cousins and Tory. Tory was the one supposedly trying to purchase it. They recognized the whip, every last one of them had the oh shit look on their face. I was back in rotation like my cousin's clothes between the closest homies. A fresh pair of blue and white Nike Dunks and a blue and gray Detroit Lions puffy starter coat, pants creased up with styrofoam, I was geared up hopping out that Cutlass. Lil Stan and I were hopping out every morning smelling like fresh like some herbal essences along with some Joop cologne. Candy was on deck. If Bro ain't have the candy, Mrs. Fordham did. It was things to look forward to going to high school, you could get all the action. It was either gym or lunch, lunch, you going to catch a dice game, card game, cats rapping at the table, and if you a player, scoring on something pretty because you bought her lunch would put you in the door. Don't get me wrong, though; after seeing a couple of demos floating throughout the building from failing a class or two, me and a couple of guys started living by the laws and policies of living righteous. We started to take education a little more serious. We would twist fingers in the hallway; some would get their squares in in the bathroom, couples would meet by the lockers, but the halls were empty.

We were 5-0 at the time as a football team. A powerhouse squad, having the GODFATHER of football as a coach, our split backfield, and the twenty eight or twenty seven special was going to get you beat every time. After preparing for Harper High school one night, rolling down 70th and Green, we were looking for some Doja. Well, well well, what do we have here? We weren't even high yet, and that blew us. Squadded up with the usual, we bumped into some of the members of Harper we were playing against the next day at Stagg Stadium, what a coincidence. Words exchanged on what was going to take place on the field the next day. High or not, we were going to smoke them. Game time at Stagg Stadium on a Saturday was always a rivalry game. Entering the locker room Coach C, mention that some of the Harper players had a screaming match on the block with us. How did we even cross paths? Coach mentioned something about us smoking that shit, sounding like the funeral director off tales from the hood, "the shit, the shit." The Robeson boys spent like $40 bucks of a big bag of huff off the block, where one of the players lived who played for Harper. They tricked on us. Guess their Coach told our Coach. That wouldn't stop us from winning the game. I had two touchdowns, and I kicked the field goal to get the win, 14-13. A one-point difference would put us even higher in the conference at 6-0, remaining undefeated.

Pretty sure they were blown away because they didn't want any smoke. I didn't want any smoke myself, as my life started to transition reluctantly. Articles from Chicago Sun-times and the Chicago Tribune wrote highly of a Robeson future star. My name would flash across the newspaper in the light of something good. I begin to get recognition locally and nationally. In the city, I was becoming a legend on the football field. Unless you have seen me riding around in my 1989 Cutlass in Dolton, I was MIA. Hmm, not really, the times I was seen, the stereotypes of how I was living before always haunted me; for the most part, I was a ghost. If I did hit the scene in an outfit not seen worn by my cousins, I might have gotten a look or two at the Thornridge vs Thornton High school game. Their basketball game was a different type of ball game. I was dabbling back and forth between City life and Suburban life. It's a difference between King High School playing against Dunbar or Thornton High School playing against Proviso West. A different type of energy and vibes. It feels like a bunch of fortunate uppity kids that have no clue about life or the streets in any instance. If you got on some bogus shoes, you ain't getting looked at, at a suburban game. You go to one of the suburban basketball games that's about to be off the chain; a pair of Havana Joes and a Marius Malone blue jean outfit will get you one of them suburb chicks unless they were into the hardcore look. It's like being black and trying to Mac to a white chick, that shit dead, you got to know how to talk to them. This is not just a one-way thing; it's vice versa trying to holler at a city chick. Better not come with no "hey, how you doing," you're a goofy. That how they were going to play you. Sad, but you gotta be like, "aye, shorty, what up," better hope that works. If you come at them the wrong way, you might as well pimp off. She going to treat you like a Goofy Mawg, is what we call them. A quick dosage of Chipolar, reflect on when you might have had to pimp off or got treated for not knowing how to come at a Chicago lady. Treated is what you are going to hear from the nearest witness of this diagnose. Just take that L my brother, take that L. Meanwhile chasing a couple of cuties pies while going to the local Wrights Barnes yard in Lansing or something my cousin John or Will put together, I was still fake messing with ole girl that had a guy, and I had a nice line-up. I thought I was a player. The season was going well, still hadn't been beat, and we were on a roll. It was games getting high wasn't a priority. However, getting lifted boosted my football superpowers. We were giving out L's. A couple of games later, Hubbard High school knocked us off our high horse. Hubbard had a squad. They had a raw quarterback by the name of Kelvin Hayden, he was a freshman, with Chuck in the backfield, Big Ben at middle linebacker backer, and a heck of Coaching Staff, Under the leadership of Coach E. Although Coach E came under the teaching of Coach C, he had his own style. They handed us an L; we didn't want any smoke. It wasn't the only L, and I got served one from the young lady I was dealing with, the one that had the guy at home. I think he had got a whiff of something fishy between his lady and I snooping around. I can't see how unless my name was randomly brought up in conversation. We didn't have cell phones back in the day, and since I had got busted with my beeper at the last school sweep, I never got another one, at least; not right then and there. The line of communication only consisted of several ways, school, house phones, or pull up. Yea, pagers existed, but that goes back to house phones, pull up, or a payphone. She hadn't been to school for about a week and a half, neither had we talked. Something was fishy. Word got around; she had some family issues. Despite the absence, school work was still required to be completed. So, for the rest of the school year, she finished from home. I had a car, and I didn't mind pulling up.

CHAPTER 11

SUPERSTAR

In my Junior year, I was making a name for myself in the city. All City's 1st team, All-State second team. You would have to see some footage to see what I was doing, I got my junior year tapes, and the senior videos, from my knowledge, are lost. I was making you cough the ball up, if I touched the football, you getting juked, and I'm scoring. I played punt return, kick return, punted, kick, kicked field goals, played safety, and on offense, I played Quarterback running back, and wide receiver. Drinking was never my forte, part of the reason I don't indulge in alcoholic beverages. I used to get super scummy. I'm talking out my body, wasn't no limit. The limit consists of you getting scum dumb diggery.

What type of top athletes partake in these events and still be in shape. I stayed in the newspaper. Hootie, John, and I hopped in my older cousin Dell Jr. 1997 thunderbird, tinted out with 2, 15in Rockford Fosgate speakers, and took a trip down to Northern Illinois University to kick it and hang out with one of our other homies, Sammy. Sammy was Squeak, cousin. I picked up the Northern Star, the University newspaper, and there I was on the front of their newspaper. I'm in high school on a college campus kicking it, you would have thought I was a freshman living in Grant South. A junior in high school, at a college party, I was way ahead of my time. All of my homies were older than me, so what they did, I did, and when we did it, we did it. Sometimes we overdid it, but what's overdoing it when this is what you do. I should have been more focused on winning that game, the game I was on the back of the College Newspaper. That was the game we lost to Dunbar High School. Dunbar was like our gatekeeper during my time. Something must be wrong with him, that's what you are thinking, and you still wondering, told you that's that Chipolar. You think we honestly would have lost that game 28 to 22 with two overtimes. I remember it like it was yesterday. The night before, I had got super drunk, and that ain't take much, but a sip or two don't hurt nobody. A fifth of absolute vodka and a couple of swishers did not allow me to reach my full potential that night against Dunbar in the final four, I jagged. Gasping for air and hoping not to throw up all over Gately's field, it was a rough night for me. I didn't stink up the field, I still manage to throw a couple of touchdowns and have some big-time runs, but I played on an empty tank. Before I called a hike, I would rest on top of my center, lay there drifting off to a sedated mind state, then click in and call the cadence. I was there, but I was out of my body. We ran the score up quickly, at half time, it was 22-8, right. Ain't no way we were supposed to lose that game, I just know, I got loaded and drunk the night before, and if I hadn't, we might have blown them off the field, should have just smoked. This isn't just no Chipolar syndrome, conscienceless yea I was, not throwing anyone under the bus, your favorite athlete was probably worse than me. And on another note, anyone will tell you, I was better than your best athlete at my worst. I had natural talent. Plus, I was elusive with the ball in my hand and would run straight through the most immense player on the field. My name stayed ringing on the intercom. My name was buzzing buzzing. That summer, I stayed on the move, receiving all types of offers to major University camps, I took it upon myself to go to Ohio State camp. I hopped on the first Greyhound smoking. The Buckeyes showed interest in me and sent me an invite. When breaking the news to my mom, she fully supported me and encouraged me to go. I booked a ticket to Ohio solo, with no chaperon. From Chicago 95th and state to Ohio, it was an 8 hr. trip on the bus. In Chicago, most athletes live a double life, grasping the concept of how to survive in the streets, in addition to the sports, you might have a future if you don't get Cocheesed. Many times, out of ten, once you left after-school activities, you headed straight to the block anyway. Your involvement in sports sometimes saves you from block activities. Unless someone embedded in your head, you're the man, and you don't know you, the man. Most athletes or even street legends, matter fact, successful people before success, radiate a light that makes them a star, whether locally or nationally.

I'm 16 years old, arriving at the Ohio State Buckeyes football summer camp, straight from the southside of Chicago; Englewood, Paul Robeson High School on 69th and Normal, this is Lionel Hickenbottom after an introduction to the head coach John Cooper. It is a good thing I did my research. I was about to put Woody Hayes, after all these years, I thought it was Woody Hayes, tweaking. I swear that man told me that was his name was Woody Hayes. This was the year Joey Galloway ran a 4.1 in a 40-second dash.

Did you come all the way here from Chicago? One of the coaches asked. "That's a long way coming down here." I'm thinking to myself, y'all sent me an invite, wasn't much talking, I let my performance speak. I went into their camp as a QB, WR, RB, DB, and did returns. At QB, I was zipping the ball, leading every wideout on their routes. At Wideout, I was killing them coming off the line with the footwork. Flipside, I'm at DB, probably one dude got off the line, and gave me a dosage of my own medicine, hit me with a slant. My athleticism, hard work, and dedication allowed me to get MVP of the Ohio State camp. That was a major accomplishment for me at that time, it officially gave me the confidence to perform at a high level.

IHSA Football released the top players in the state leading up to the season. I had gained a spot as one of the top all-purpose players in Illinois. My stats were impeccable, I was putting up numbers. Seeing myself in the newspaper was normal, front page or back. Never did I let it go to my head. This little badass dude, in the eyes of authority, had switch the narrative. I had too much going on to get myself in any type of trouble, I was playing it safe, not saying I wouldn't indulge in any activity. I was motivated to do something great after receiving the honor of MVP at Ohio State University. Coach C had a stable career in the NFL and had connections throughout the football world. About a week into school, senior year, he pulls me in the office, sits me down, and have me fill out an NFL prospect form. Would I be the first high school football player to go straight to the National Football League? Yes, I sound crazy as hell, yes, I took a bunch of hits to the head, I'm fucked up, probably got CTE, just talking shit, but Hecky yea filling out that form, I thought I was going to straight to the league, and teammates did too. Chipolar like a motherfucker.

Word started spreading like a wildfire about the opportunity to play football professionally right after high school, I told one of the guys, and he told the whole school and hood. Royalty treatment was suitable for a very important person like me and on top of the Aid and Assist, I felt like Prince Akeem off Coming to America. I was interviewing ladies, searching for Lisa. Had a couple of women trying to claim me like Lisa's sister, as if I was Darryl or Semmi. I wasn't going. I wanted me a Lisa McDowell-type lady. Meanwhile, my high school crush had a little pudge. Could my opportunity for the NFL still withstand? I thought that might have sent her off and she saw an opportunity to detour my route on the path to greatness. But that wasn't the case. A simple high and bye and a couple of cold shoulders alerted me she wasn't Lisa, and I wasn't Prince Hakeem. The thoughts of me being a teenage dad fade away swiftly, quick. Focusing on football ball and being the first high school ballplayer to go pro was my goal. That goal was set high, wasn't it?

I worked my ass off that summer, pertaining to football. On the field, you saw it, I wasn't letting up. I was a superstar. How do you maintain that stardom, and you haven't even made it yet? Do you think a young man from the Southside of Chicago could go play pro ball at the age of 17 or 18? Is he built like that? You couldn't tell me I wasn't! Educational wise as a student-athlete, the biggest misconception is that you don't have to focus on doing your schoolwork or passing a test. Why? Cause you a Jock, you going pro, everybody loves you, and you have the charisma to go with it. I think that's the biggest misconstrued message to any athlete that's looking to play any level of sports is to not maintain a high GPA. How else will you be able to showcase your athleticism besides recreational? My senior year was challenging in the classroom. I didn't realize how much in my younger days I fucked off in the classroom room. I was behind. My grades on paper would probably give me a hard time trying to get into Kennedy King Community College. But why would I focus on grades if I was going straight to the league, good question, right?

This type of method is a rare case. Honestly, at that time I didn't know what the NFL was, I thought Ohio State, Alabama, Notre Dame, and Florida State were playing professionally, because it was more exciting. Yea, I grew up knowing about the NFL through playing games like techno bowl and watching it on TV, but what child dreams of just playing for the NFL before the Rolling tide. Life after high school for me, I wouldn't need any education, just give me the money; the ultimate set up for failure, and to any athlete with that mentality, salute. You better know how to read and write, if not, you going to be the first one to get jerked out of your money. Some type of education, especially going from high school to professional ball, no college. I wasn't dumb, and I wasn't any fool, it was just when it came to school, I wasn't the brightest student, trying to be smart and nerdy just wasn't embedded in me. Now I have been through something's I realized I'm a genius, but any who. Visitation from top universities began to roll in, some of the first questions asked, what type of student is he? How are his grades? Did he take the ACT or SAT yet? I wasn't on top of neither one of those. Meanwhile, wasn't anyone in the history of Paul Robeson High School during my days before or after that had Mrs. Melton ever walked the stage and received their diploma if you didn't pass her class. She pulled me to the side and let it be known, she would fail me in a heartbeat. She wasn't playing either. I had to get on it, I had business to take care of, University of Tennessee offers me a full ride but asked have I taken the ACT. I don't even know what an ACT was.

CHAPTER 12

BALLIN

On the field, I was killing, putting up stat after stat my senior year, we were undefeated first five games, I wasn't getting beat. Yea, ok, between goofing off my grades early on in high school, not having grades, unprepared for an ACT, all I need is an 18, and I could play at the next level, I was losing. Not graduating and taking my talents to the next level was not an option. My aunt told me about Mr. McNabb ACT and Sat Tutoring services. Although Mr. McNabb had his son on his way to play professional ball at the time, he was helping young student-athletes prepare for the test of their life. I think I was just going through the motions, acting like I was reciprocating the information all the time, I had a lot of focusing to do. That focus required getting on the right track. First, focusing on the belligerent statements about not graduating if I didn't pass Mrs. Melton English class ignited my fire. Preparing for the ACT, I needed more time, I should have paid a little more attention in class growing up. To some people, the test was easy breezy, not for me. Mr. McNabb gave me pinpoints on managing my time and answering the questions to the best of my ability. My ability to get majority of the questions right was incomprehensible. Now understand, out of three tries, I tried every method a successful ACT taker ah take. I had one of my closest friends go in the day of the test high and drunk and got a 28 out of 36 on it. He, by far, was one of the smartest dumb guys that I know. The man said every time he went in there to test, it was from a night before of smoking and drinking. I know he was in there loaded. I tried every method anyone can tell you, all the way down to just circling C. I think the first time I went to test, I went sober. Sometimes the odds can be working against you, but what's the chances a smart guy like me scoring a 14 out of 36. The devastation was written all over my face when I got those results, damn it, Lionel, I thought you were smarter than that. You get a bunch of points just writing your name on the piece of paper, sheesh.

A 14 on the American College Testing tells a lot about a kid when trying to play for a big-time University. The minimum score to receive a full-ride scholarship, you need at least an 18. The next time I went, I answered the questions to the best of my ability, about a quarter more to finished all C's I thought would be correct. I scored even lowered, landing a 13. I begin to question my ability. I had the ball skills, but did I had the IQ level to compete? That test made me feel like I was dumb, comparing myself to my friends' magnificent score of 28, the first time, 26 the second time, and a 29 the third time. All while being drunk and high. With one more chance to get an 18, I was left with only one option. Granted, I was doing good in my school work, but I took a fond time trying to get my grades and GPA right. I was doing great in Mrs. Melton's class, I ain't have a choice I was trying to graduate on time. Big time Universities were still coming to visit. We had a successful season, going into the second round of the state playoffs, losing to Mattoon high school. Any athlete with a bright future, when growing up, you don't know what you sign up for. You just try out and if you are good, you make the squad, the political side of it, your name all in the newspaper, name all on the intercom, getting invited to do interviews, no way to prepare unless you come from that type of background. I'm speaking for athletes from the Southside of Chicago or neighborhood that is identical with the same systematic structure on how they breed and structure an athletic star's future. It's not many resources to reach from. Not many of us catch on.

The whole NFL form I filled out was just inspiration, Coach never explained to me what it consists of, maybe he did line my future up for me. I just need to take initiative to the only ones going straight to the pros out of high school to play professional ball were NBA players. Coach pulled me into the office and started discussing my real future in football. I had a shoebox full of letters to any university across the United States of America, except Florida State. Coach 1st option to play at a collegiate level, Jackson State University. No good. I had nothing against Jackson State, but just wasn't my interest, I have never seen them on the major TV networks.

When I did catch a game of Jackson State, it was almost like Simeon High school vs. CVS high school. It was like a CPS game, us on National TV. I was use to the traditional football look, the games on TV, crowds going bananas, the players showboating. Most folks, unless you just straight SWAC, you enjoy watching a game of Alabama vs Georgia. The average kid's hopes and dreams of playing college football at one of these two programs are no different from Rudy the movie. That movie just gave so much confidence to a player with not even half as much talent as I had. A guy like Rudy pretty much got the grades but had no talent in the coach's eyes in real life. On the flip side, you got talent but can't get the grades. I just knew I belong on the big stage. Being on the big stage requires doing the little things along the way to properly prepare yourself to do bigger things. It began to sink in, something I never dreamed of or even desired to have, it had me over emotionally. My opportunities had been cut short when I thought it was cool to say fuck school, my freshman year, sophomore, and junior year. Here it is I'm a senior given an opportunity, and I couldn't run away with it. I didn't have a chance. Goofing off my first couple of years affected me being able to showcase my talents on the Georgia and Alabama level. I still had one more to the good to pass the ACT and play some ball. After bombing it twice and going in with a sober mind, realizing that didn't work, the next test day, I got loaded. I know we all different, and I keep referring to my homie who Aced it with flying colors high and drunk, let me know it was possible. I just smoked a blunt, and I was focused. I felt good about it, couldn't tell me I ain't pass. The score came back, got a 12. Don't call me dumb, just say I didn't apply myself cause I'm smart as motherfucker. I'm just going to say I wasn't a good test taker, ya dig.

Earlier that summer, while playing 7on7, Coach S from Northern Illinois University came to check us out at Washington park on 55th. It was pouring down that day, I remembered vividly, he introduced himself and showed interest. He also popped up at the school extending that offer to play at NIU. I never in a million years heard of the NIU football team, I use to go up there and kick it, that's about it. I was caught up in the big programs. After conversing with Coach S, he found out I wasn't eligible or even going to have the grades to go to school. He explained a program named C.H.A.N.C.E at NIU, and I should look into it more. Coach C and I had to agree to a disagreement on me even considering NIU. During those years lot of Chicago ballplayer went down south, it's tradition with all the connections and politics in the Inner city. Alumni are a big part of that. I honestly didn't believe I would thrive at Jackson St. I had homie went down there, and when he came back one summer, fam wasn't right. I was willing to accept the challenge of the diverse culture, he knew I grew up around Filipinos, Latins and Caucasions. I was immune to the cultural shock. That night Coach S and the head Coach of NIU stop by my parents to let them know how much they wanted me to attend their program. Coach S did majority of the talking, he sold the program. Coach N, the head coach showed interest, but I could tell he was hesitant. He didn't know what to think, here it is I go to Robeson High School on 69th and Normal, but you meet me at my parents home in

Dolton. Mind-boggling, Coach S got it, whether they had to pull up on 67th and Aberdeen, he was willing to risk his life to get talent. I might not did too well in the classroom, but my family had class. The invitation from Coach S and Coach N was life changing. If you ever been on a recruitment visit to a school you thinking about going to play a sport, it's love. Oh, they going to do any and everything to get you to come to their program. You going to have a good ass time. I took the visit, for me, it was nothing to just go crazy over. Mainly the reason being is because how I was moving around at home in the streets. Plus, I went down there during the winter break, so it wasn't that many people there. They assigned a player to monitor us. I forget who was my player, but we pretty much just chilled. Ended up over one of the older player houses, it was a couple of big girls there, I was cool. I got me some smoke, I felt like I was back at home with the guys. Later got back to my room and start tweaking just a little bit, hoping they weren't going to trick on me.

They ain't say nothing, I fell right in to place. Coach S went more into depth about the route I need to take. To them attainable, to me afar. They wanted me to come in through the chance program, sit out my first year and be a Prop 48. Prop 48, basically you can't play your first year in college you are considered ineligible. Not passing that ACT, not taking high school seriously, my first couple years were important. No one growing up while I was playing little league or even an OG in the streets ever told me, how to maintain what I was good at. It was normal for me to see the dopest athlete in the hood to be smoking a blunt or drunk off thier rocket, but it's like it enhanced it or something when it came to ballin. They ain't tell me to evolve and go to the next level, be smart. I was smart, just off instincts and survival mode, but they prey down upon guys that were nerdy like or trying to be on some smart shit. Honestly you wasn't looked at as being cool when you were on some nerd shit and didn't take up for yourself, and people just bullied you. Like many of us from Chicago, we are steered in a direction that can lead us down the wrong path. I was eager to correct my shit, I was always trying to walk righteously.

CHAPTER 13

PROM

As my senior started to finish up, it came to the realization we had to move on. Early out, a lot of people had moved on well before graduation. People laugh all the time when I tell them how many of us graduated from high school. I would be glad to say I was one of 43. Yea I passed Mrs. Melton's class. In those last high school days, I was focused on what school I was going to go to, if any. My mother and father had a big fallout because my pops didn't think it was in my best interest to go to college. That man sent it up, "he aint going to no motherfucking college, the boy needs to get a job." Pop says. I'm just sitting there quiet, I really ain't know what to say, my mama wasn't trying to hear it. Pops was a hard-working man; I don't know why he ain't want me to go to school and play ball. I don't think he saw the bigger picture. Things had calmed down, and prom was a couple of weeks away. I had already decided I wasn't going to go. I was straight, I just felt like I was too cool for that shit. I had already gone to the two previous proms, so I already know how they went. Granted, it was my prom but, I felt like I wasn't missing anything. There was no way my friends were going to let me skip out on prom. The day of prom I decided I was going to go; I hadn't prepared not one minute. I was making the decision that day of, and it required little preparation. I had a free tux at the local men's warehouse, I took full advantage. They had my tux ready within a couple of hours, it was rented, but hey, it would do. The next thing I would have to worry about is the whip. What car would I drive, how would I get there? I could have easily asked one of the closest homies to barrow they whip to ride in style, you know, probably a Chevy on 22's, a Benz, or a Range Rover. At this time, my pops were feeling a little generous. The man offers me to ride his 1997 Cadillac Deville. Man, he barely rode it. It stayed parked in the garage and got bought out on the sunny days or the days he felt like pushing it. Grown man toy with the 17in vogues. I'm talking about, super clean, sunroof with leather interior. Pops ain't play about his whips, couldn't even play around them. Boy, he would snap. But I felt him. Memorabilia moment pops threw me the keys and said, "son, you can push the lac to prom." I tried to play it all cool cause I had mixed feelings. Excitement, overwhelming, paranoia, astound, and yes quite shocking, that he would let me drive his 1997 Cadillac Deville. Later, that day, the tux came in, I went with the all-white, with Forrest green, to add some coloring. I was clean as a whistle. Pops sent me off in class, sunroof back, 17in vogues on beam, and I'm blasting "Do you wanna ride in the back seat of the caddy" by Do or Die ft. Twista. Had it on repeat, hoping the CD ain't scratch, blasting it you could hear ever word with them tweeters. I ended up leaving a little early and pulled up on 73rd and Lowe to my homie Dae Dae crib.

We had mobbed-up over there, all the fellas and their dates, this where the pregame would take place before prom. We were pretty much just chilling out, and pictures were taken that would capture the moment. Senior year we kept a tight- knit group, and those that were squad decided to ride out from Dae Dae's. We were at least seven cars deep on our way to prom. Swerving in out of traffic, you saw us coming, and every senior whose prom it was, was Downtown. For all parents, the night of prom often causes stress. Prom night, anything goes, let's be honest unless you are just super lame and avoid all conflicts, and your parents make sure of that. Somethings that can happen prom night! Daughter, cherries getting popped, drunk driving, a whole lot of hate, and an open ball game with little to no parental guidance on a young adult night. We pulled up in the same formation trailed from 73rd to prom, with a sort of club like vibe, pulling up dead smack in the front, hopping out our vehicles to small talk, that's how you stunted. Sometimes stunting can go wrong in all the wrong places. We had maintained the same order route to prom from 73rd and Lowe to Deep downtown. So, the person driving in front of me was always the same, it wasn't like anything change once we found out where we were supposed to park. Heading to the parking deck, which was upstairs, head straight that way, were the valet words, pointing in the direction of go. All I can remember is the homie in front of me hit reverse. The last thing I wanted to happen had just manifested in a blink of the eye. "Boom," that's all you heard.

My head went down, shaking it in the motion of No, my heart went to my privates. I was fucked, the first thought came to mind, "what the fuck." Million-dollar question? Why did he bag the car back? I have no idea. My prophetic instincts told me not to go to prom, for some odd reason, I didn't even want to go, decided the day of. Then this happens, a car accident in front of prom, that was a great way to kick off the prom night. My night was doomed, I could hear pops right now. I could not enjoy myself, went upstairs to prom, word had spread like a wildfire. I was trying to figure out how I would tell my ole man I had just got into a minor car accident, and he was missing a headlight. By far felt like one of the hardest things to do. That didn't play about his car. The only thing that could make me feel good at this point was a blunt. Sad right, but what else was going to ease my mind. One of my homegirls' boyfriends was thee savior, we hit the rooftop and touched the sky. That was the only way to clear my mind, by the time I hit the blunt, I was ready to face the "motherfucker bring my car home right now" statement, "before I kick yo ass," response from my father. Afterward, it is getting around how down I was, one of the teachers decides she would call my father. That made me feel a little better, at least he wouldn't curse me out in front of her or send threats, where it would raise suspicions to her. I know he would be pissed off to the max, however. This was back when we had caller ID, whatever name he saw on the screen, he picked it up on the first ring. You could tell he was already on point. Hello, "Hi, Mr. Hickenbottom, this Mrs. Moon over here at Paul Robeson high school." She explained to him how she heard how he would respond because of the accident, and she just wanted him to know it wasn't my fault and didn't want him to blow it out of proportion. Man, she controlled the vibe because pops was extra cool and asked was I ok. Unusual response than some scenarios before. He wasn't even tripping, and I was able to enjoy the little prom I had left.

CHAPTER 14

HIGH SCHOOL GONE

Approaching graduation meant locking in on completing some major assignments, especially Mrs. Melton's class. She didn't care who you were, superstar, gangbanger, drug dealer, or whatever she wanted to see you succeed. And if you had a relationship with someone trying to help you win in life, better question your integrity and dignity. She was like your Auntie, your Moms or Granny, but she was a great teacher with great intention. I use to think she wanted to see us fail, no lie. Most of the time, people see things in you, you haven't discovered. Although she saw the potential in her students, she also brought it out of them. It was challenging even to make it to my senior year and having a glimpse of what playing college football would be like. If I could just graduate and go straight pro, kudus for the ones that did do it; baseball and basketball-wise, I don't think anyone ever done it football-wise. You couldn't tell me I wasn't going to be the first, that's how raw I thought I was, but I honestly got sent off by Coach C filling out that NFL prospect form at an early age. Besides, I had to prepare for it. Lesson one, I think every student-athlete being developed to further their careers at the next level shall be groomed to speak in a politically correct manner when doing public speaking. A couple of interviews and meetings cannot prepare a young child from an inner-city throughout the world to speak to the world. Most superstar athletes from inner cities with cameras and microphones shoved in their face, is their onsite training from there. In the final assembly, class of 2000 Robeson, I had an opportunity extended from Mrs. Melton about being the MC of the last program. I said no, but apparently, that meant yes, in other words, I had no choice. Anyone that has ever Mc'd or hosted a large event pertaining to public speaking, there is an art. I had to learn that art quickly. I was given a script written out in correspondence in leading us into a productive future. I just had to make sure I was on point. The night before and throughout the day, I read through the script to make sure I could pronounce all words. Timing and a good delivery are the tools utilize for this great picture drawn out. Before the assembly, I was given a pep talk from the Assistant Principal on how I better not mess this opportunity up. I'm thinking to myself, I didn't ask for it. I had to perform, like anything else, I nailed it, did a good ass job. I was hitting them with punchlines, reading off the script, cracked a couple of jokes, was no way I was going to embarrass myself. You know how many people had a problem reading in front of the class, imagine the whole school. I was probably a knucklehead, but I wasn't dumb. I was one of the smart ones, not to say people who haven't completed High school are not better off than a person who has, statistically wise where I am from not many young Indigneous Gods focus is school. I started off as one of them but began to gain interest in getting some knowledge or just not feeling dumb when I'm out and about. Street smarts and school smarts are a dangerous combination. So being a graduate of the class of 2000 was memorabilia. In my freshman year, 400 students were enrolled, upon graduation, 43. I was one of these 43 students to cross the stage. You talking about memorabilia, this wasn't your typical graduation. Visually speaking, think about any graduation you attended, it was in some of auditorium, gymnasium, or even a church, our graduation took place dead smack in the parking lot of Robeson high school. Yes, 6800 Normal Avenue. Any familiarity with Paul Robeson High School's area in conjunction with Englewood high school innerstands the dynamic of the war between territories. In this area, it's interchangeable, which means the GD'S and the BD'S are mixed in. The conversation being held of, was it safe to graduate on the parking lot where rival gangs could have a shoot-out. Or not even a shoot-out, just come through and disrespect the whole demonstration. Something to think about, peacefully, we were sent out with class.

Allow someone to spread their wings. So many of us with limited resources are not valued and often seek validation outside of selves. Tough love is what we're built off of in most inner cities. Lot of hooting and hollering. It's not shown in affection early onto see what love is early on, and we often fall victim to hating everything about ourselves. I was feeling this way often, but I was given a chance to continue to do something I loved, and that's playing college ball.

I had made the all-star team my senior year and was looking to broadcast my talents in the last game of the CPS career. My main focus wasn't the Allstar game, I had already made a name for myself, they knew I was a baller. I was looking forward to my orientation visits at NIU. Northern Illinois University took a liking to me as a student-athlete and wanted to bring my talents to their school. NIU has a CHANCE program that helps students with a low GPA attend their school. I had to take that route; I knew I had to take that route. Coach S explained to me that I would have to enter through this program, maintain a GPA of 2.5 my freshman year, and the following year I would receive a scholarship. No other school took a chance on me after pulling my grades and GPA, including my ACT scores.

On my first day of freshman orientation, I felt a little out of place as I stayed to myself. Although we were all coming in the same route, all the same age, I was a little more advance, so far as politicking with anyone, I rather just kept quiet. Looking like a D boy fresh off the street in the corner, I knew it was some judgmental folks at a non-HBCU school. How is a 17-year older rocking two chains, got on Iceberg clothing, and super smooth, finds himself on a University campus? Let them tell it I belong on the block conducting some business as us street dudes do. Right! During my orientation, I had befriended two ladies, that was pretty, I'm talking super pretty. They caught a whiff of a player, I guess. Exploring the campus with two beautiful ladies, shade started to come from every angle. We had a night where we all sat around and gave our background. Mind you we were being chaperon by two guys that were upperclassmen. I don't know where they were from, but they look just like me. I'm 17, they were like 22 or 23. The difference is, I wasn't no little ass boy, and they knew that by my demeanor. I guess by them being upper classmen, they were trying to flex for the incoming freshmen ladies, damn creeps. By the time they got to me and ask me my background, and what I wanted to major in, everything got chaotic. My reply when asked what I wanted to study, I simply replied, "I'm here to play football." Only this I thought would be major, if I went pro. At the end of the conversation, most humbly without hostility, the college tour guide tells me, "You won't make it here," and he meant it, what a dickhead. Coming from where we from and having to work on self-confidence, I felt mine had just been stripped. These the same cats, you can tell by the way they dressed, they were some Doofuses. They just both look like they stunk. They thought they were shitting on me, but I was going to make them smell me. That remark always stuck with me. The two young ladies had rocked out with me for the rest of the orientation, showing me nothing but love. They had no idea I was a Top Athlete throughout the land.

Meanwhile, as the orientation wrapped up and we were about to go home, I offered the two young ladies a ride back to Chicago. It was more feasible for me to hop on the greyhound and go home. Ticket use to be anywhere between

$15 bucks and $25. I was press with time headed back to the city. It was All-star weekend for CPS football, and we had a banquet that Friday night leading up to game-time. On the way back home, my mom and the two young ladies hit off well. We caught vibe and talked about the fall school year. What a coincidence they both lived nearby in the south suburbs. We made a stop at the banquet so I could be acknowledged for my football skills throughout my high school year. What's a better way to roll into a banquet with your mom dukes, and two beautiful ladies and the answer the two girls give when asked "who are they?' Hysterically their response is, "we are his girlfriends." Must be the classic answer. My cheekbones were hurting, I was smiling so hard. From ear to ear. High five and daps as if I score a touchdown off the opening kick-off return was shown as respect. I had gained some confidence back from them two creeps back at the college campus, who was hating on a young playa. Allstar game, I got my rocks off, well, not really, I felt like I was trying to get more outdone and was shun. CPS schools that year had some good ballplayers that committed to schools accepting a full-ride scholarship. At that time, I think the most prestigious school someone attended was the University of Tennessee. Although I was one of the most talented to come out of Chicago, NIU was the only school that took a chance on me. So many inner-city children miss their opportunity to further their careers, not just because of a piss poor environment, but for having piss poor grades. You know how many Michael Jordans it is that never see the court due to the lack of grades. I explain to the younger generation the importance of taking care of that business in the classroom. Many think that just because they have talent, it will allow them to participate in a sport. But, nope, that's not the case, well, in most cases, not mine.

CHAPTER 15

NIU

Fall school year had rolled around, and I was officially leaving home to go to college, it was surreal. I was the first one out of my family to leave home and go to college. I had prepared all of my things, and as the days got closer, I questioned my confidence, was I built for a school? It wasn't so much of the school thing, I believe it was more about transitioning into something great. You are rarely given a vision to see outside your norm when you have never seen anything other. It was a lot of more prepared students than I was, I kind of felt like it would be better to learn more about the streets. The day of leaving to go off to college was bitter-sweet. I was officially leaving my old ways behind, something I've known so well. Besides hanging out at NIU my junior and senior year, the only glimpse of real college was the movie "The Program." Moms hit the back road to Dixie Highway, hopped on 294 to i88. Along the ride, things begin to sink in, I was now entering a new dimension in my life. What an ole suburban/city boy knows about going away to college, living life on campus, and no supervision. The no supervision part, I was used to that, but adapting to a university environment was foreign. I didn't know anyone, and I hadn't run into the two ladies who rode back home with me from orientation. That first day was pretty much just me adjusting. When I hit campus, I had got settled in, my mom's gave me my farewell, that good ole mama talks with a powerful prayer, and I was officially out of the bird's nest. Figuratively speaking, my mom is not a bird. I just had a Chipolar moment. We often tweak like that we think that deep, like how I just went that deep to think that whoever is reading this instantly thought my mom is bird brain just because I said I left the bird nest. I did and flocked to my own nest, and it all started in Grant South dormitory.

On the 11th floor, A-side, grant south, the Architect you would have thought they plagiarized a Chicago high-rise project building. It had a similar design. I hadn't traveled but probably an hour and 15 minutes away from home, but it felt like we were right down the street. Often running into characters with the same resemblance of one of the guys or females I've known for some time, my character never changed. The transition to just this big-time jock didn't just take place right off back for me. That first day of college felt like a month wrapped up in 24 hrs. My roommate and I had clicked right away, like a 1st cousin relationship. He was cool, and where he was from, he was the man on the field, but he had to be a prop 48 his freshman year just like I did. What's a prop 48? Prop 48 mandates that for a student-athlete to qualify to play in Division I athletics as a freshman, the athlete must carry a minimum 2.0-grade point average (GPA) in 11 core courses and a combined 700 score on the SAT. I was already enrolled off a prayer and a wish, and learning how to navigate the campus and finding how to get to my first class was a task within itself. I was learning as I was going.

I did plug with one good guy during orientation, that wasn't trying hard to fit in with the inner crowd. If anything, he was trying to snatch up one of those hotties I had on the side of me and spit some knowledge to me about how we were Geniuses. A couple of G code words, I knew one day we would be Aiding and Assisting each other one day in some righteous endeavors. Tony Tone was straight from Chicago, loud, smart, ignorant, and a fucking genius. We plugged for a reason.

Next couple days, I eventually ran into one of the women I had met on orientation, the vibes were a little different. I wasn't tripping, it was more a comfort zone, well I would say friend zone. You could tell she was like one the finest girls in high school, and what happens at school stay at school, because you had the RK's before RK, hitting on them. It was pointless to have a car around campus, so when her boyfriend pulled up on the 22in rims on a SS, looking like money, you checked yourself as if you were there to get a degree. Two days had gone pass now, classes hadn't started, after attending a couple of festivities and chilling in my dorm room, I started to get homesick.

This isn't nothing but the second day, reality began set in. What was I doing here? I just came from the last 11 years running through the Chicagoland area, going from a boy to a young man, which felt like to me, yesterday. At this given moment, it was bigger than football, G, I wasn't even a part of the football team at this time. Did I have the mental capacity to endure the repetition of even becoming a student? I could be so much more if I were back home, but what would I even be doing back home? You know how sometimes you can envision whatever you were trying to envision. If I had visualized me going back home, it would have been me forcing it. All I was focused on was getting on the field and playing some football. It still didn't dawn on me; I was there to get an education.

CHAPTER 16

GETTING EDUCATED

All that horse playing I did in school during my elementary, middle, and high school affected me in the school system. One thing I can say is that I learned a lot in the streets of Chicago. I'm talking about preparing you for a real-life situation. During high school, I did get a glimpse of what it was like to learn somewhat or at all; being a productive student, but not in repetition, where it was habitual. So, that first day of class, I felt like a flunky. I walked into class, and it was a class class. The desk was neat and in order, the class filled with about 20 students, and the first time in my career as a U.S. Student, I felt like I was about to be schooled. "Famo, what up, G? Boy, you in this class?" Tony Tone came out of nowhere to make sure he acknowledged a real one. I thought I was back at the Robe hearing, bro, as if we grew up together. All walks of life learned on the campus of Northern Illinois University. The Chance program provided that for many students who lacked the qualification of the university academic standards due to low G.P.A or ACT/SAT scores.

What college campus you know with a Harold's Chicken on campus? Come on now, how real does it get. When you saw people or things that reminded you of home, that's what made that chance all worth it. The first day of class is always going to be a breeze. Introducing yourself and giving a narrative on your background can be an easy assignment in conjunction with the hindsight of future goals discussed. A 10 AM class, next class at 6:30 PM, I had to be crazy to think every day was this sweet. I was taking 15 credit hours. My Tuesdays and Thursdays let me know I wasn't going to have that much time as I thought, after Monday's schedule. It began to feel like college college. Class assignments and having a social life were balanced; going straight nerd wasn't an easy transition. I wasn't quite a student-athlete, and my restriction didn't have any limit. Indulging in a smoke session with a couple of people was scarce, for some odd reason, someone would get to tweaking and blow my high. I was discreet when it came to smoking, it was a habit for me, a sense of security to help me face my slow process of adjusting to an all-out student. I hadn't even enrolled in a foriegn class, and already my math class was looking foreign. I was struggling to grasp the task of, I needed to be passing my classes to play football.

What an obstacle! not easy to complete, at least not for me. What's so oblivious to the fact in all actuality, all levels of education are easy, and if you apply yourself, you can get all

A's, at least B's, super facts. All you must do is turn your work in, do your research and answer the questions correctly. At the end of the week or semester, the test is the information from previous assignments. Study, study, study. I knew some people who never even attended class, showed up on test day, and passed the test with flying colors. They had the nerve to be the first ones to finish while I'm over there struggling to conjure up information stored in my brain, I thought I stored. I was probably thinking too hard. Dropping some jewels for some young folks who's thinking about going to college. First, your professor is a person, meaning a person, just like you. They put they pants on the same way as the next.

Outside of class, most professors party harder than an average student who fell into the party life of a rockstar. But don't get it twisted, it's not what you do it's how you do it. So, take care of your business. Second, talk to them, communicate, allow them to learn your name. With, when it's time to give out grades and they are going down their grade book, see understand, so many people must get A's, B's, C's, D's, and F's. If they know you and you haven't been that productive, but still put forth the effort, they won't give you an F. Third, the first day they give you the syllabus, the syllabus consists of the class layout and assignments. The first day your teacher gives you your first assignment, which will probably be due 2 to 3 weeks from that date, complete it as soon as possible. Completing it as soon as possible allows you to proofread or change some answers that you might have gotten wrong if you are not hooked up with the right study group. Fourth, attendance plays a major part unless you are just a genius and you don't need to show up to class, just turn in work and pass all tests. If you know about habits as I do, make those repetitive. You could be the first one from where you from, or look like I look, been through something and seen what I saw and be valedictorian or Salutatorian. I thought I was doing right, or at least passing, I showed up every day, but I wasn't reciprocating the syllabus nor getting help from a study group. I was just going off the strength. I wasn't strong enough mentally. I only passed 3 out of 5 classes, I was placed on academic probation. It was challenging.

Winter break being back home and finding out through a mailed letter from the counselor and the dean of office, my chances that were given was looking slim—a 1.9 GPA. I need a 2.0 GPA to be eligible to play football.

Technically yes, I was kicked out of school after the first semester. An extended break was not in the plans. I wasn't trying to get too comfortable at home, I was getting used to my little shoebox-size dorm room. You heard about the stories about never seeing someone again after the first semester. Many times, out of 10, they partied or just weren't equipped for school and said, fuck it. Either it got worse, to not getting back in and getting off probation, or they just completely gave up. Communication goes a long way. My mother and I were headed down to Dekalb a day earlier to talk with my counselor about my options, one, not being flunked out and back active in the hood. The light was at the end of the tunnel. I will be honest, I never believe I was there to get an education. Underestimating the value of the longevity in it, the light was not illuminating the tunnel. It was me getting on that field, the crazy part about it, education was the only way I would be able to showcase my talent. At least I had something kicking me in my ass to get on the right track. I was given another chance, my second semester.

Ahh, Sukie Sukie now, I was front row in my 8:30 class, like what up. A tutor, some proper preparation, and I were on top of my assignments as soon as I got them. Papers usually turned in with grammatical and punctuation errors, was corrected, my professors knew I was trying to ball out next season. I got a couple of points for joining the discussion in class, but for the most part, if I got a 70%, which was a C, I was cool. No contact, no communication with the football team was part of the restrictions as a prop 48. Redshirt freshman's that stayed back for the away games, I got familiar with, they already had a foot on the field. All my talking about what I could do on the field was just speculation. I had to first get on the field. My only problem was getting eligible. Passing these 15 hours' worth of classes was the only thing I needed to be focused on. Getting away with telling this redbone I played for the team, I think back, now, I understand manifestation. I had to speak it into existence cause she knew I wasn't even a redshirt. Any time my redshirt homie Sonny would come around, he would vouch for me. He was from Florida.

CHAPTER 17

FRESHMEN

Gold slugs all in his grill, I would joke with him and call him Florida boy. Sonny was cool with me calling him that but was quick to tell me I was green as fuck. Florida people, I didn't take it as disrespect, it's all good, I know it's equivalent to lame- ass or goofy mawg. It's all good because he became my brother. We were on a hunt trying to rip something every other night quick. One weekend, they had an away game, Sonny, and I ran into the second girl I had met during the orientation.

Let's be honest, I didn't know her, but I wouldn't mind getting to. In college I don't think nobody trying to get booed up, though. I wasn't trying to save her; she was off more than weed when I ran into her. She said something out the side of her mouth, all I know I had to show her I wasn't green, no lame, or no goofy. The ultimate disrespect, that Chipolar kicked in. We both had it. All I know is she spit on me, and with me being the competitor I am, my hock was bigger.

A dramatic snort from the pits of my nose and the back of my throat, mixed with mucus, stuck like a piece of cheese thrown at a bald head off a tik tok video. The instance of regret for attempting to spit on this guy got her embarrassed. "G, you just spit on shorty you wild as hell, yo ass crazy boi, she tried to spit on you though, you just got her ass." Tony Tone says. "Bet she won't try to treat nobody else," my boy said. I felt a sense of guilt that was low down and dirty. Some might say I was wrong some might say I was right, and she got what she deserved. They say you can take a child out of Chicago but can't take the Chicago out of the child. Academic probation wasn't the only thing I violated, but a woman who later I would date for quite some time. Chipolar is real, and we had to both have it if I'm telling you that we were messing around later on. That's another story in itself. Actions speak louder than words. I will be the first one to admit, and it's safe to say, I was just unconscious. I was operating at a frequency that didn't match the college student that wasn't on Academic probation, more like a flunky. I struggled to overcome every obstacle thrown my way after apologizing to the young lady regarding the spitting incident and feeling sorry. I began to become conscious of the moves I was making from there on out. The change was coming, but it doesn't happen overnight. My light was still lit, and that's what my motivation was to continue to shine. At this point, I was just going along with the flow of things. Class, partying, working out at the recreational center, kicking it at the dorms, and exploring the campus, was still so surreal. My college was some cool shit. It was a campus full of Chipolar people, but every Chipolar individual had an ulterior motive, whether you were to get educated or uneducated. I didn't have all the answers but surely made it a point to get everything right to stay on a path to success.

The second semester was winding down, I was crossing my T's, dotting my I's, and doing the same for my J's. Being on point was an understatement. Eligibility was at the tip of my finger, 15 credit hours, and I would be on the field in no time showcasing my talents. When I tell you, if it isn't one thing, it's two or three. Several things I look back on that built my character along the way. For some odd reason, giving up has never been the answer, everything just expires. Good thing I still had time. I'm telling you don't nothing come sweet. A week to turn in my English pro-folio, I had popped in my floppy disk on my computer, "this disk is not readable, error." I was fucked, I was panicking, the devil was a lie. Shit sent me into a state of failure. Not only did I have finals to worry about, but this was a test, I did not prepare for. So, I made two phone calls. One to Coach S and the other one to my homie Tony Tone. This phone call to Coach went something like this, "what's up buddy?" "Nothing much," coach, I replied. "Aye, coach, check this out, man this shit ain't for me, I'm probably going to head back home, I just lost my whole damn English portfolio that consists of 8 papers, each one of them four pages or better, my longest paper was ten pages." Coach with the humblest respond,

"Hey man, don't worry, calm down, fuck man, what happened?" I told him what had happened to the floppy disk, told him it was the final assignment for my English class, and he knew I had hit a brick wall. So, the second phone call to the homie, help me run right through that brick wall. From day 1 one, I knew he was going to be fam. My boy Tony Tone made one phone call.

Tony Tone asks! "Bro, do you have all your paper?" Just to inform you of this last assignment. For this assignment, I had to grammatically correct all the papers I had completed for the semester and turn them in for my final grade. Something mysterious happens to my floppy disk where it would not allow me to pull up any file I ever saved. Those that have experienced this, whether in college, high school, or job-related, know-how doomed you feel when you go to open up a floppy disk and discover it's been damaged. My homie, to this day, I thank him for helping me out at a crucial time in my life. This event is a timeline moment that I refer to when I have a moment like a flashback Friday. I met bro in the lobby of our dorm, bro walked upstairs to the B-side 9th floor.

Get off the elevator, soon as you get off the elevator, you see a big ass cloud nine sign. What a coincidence! Things often come in signs and symbols. He had arranged something with a guy on the floor to retype every one of my papers for a couple of grams of some good ole Mary. I had explained to the guy what had happened, and he said no problem. Before he even got started, a couple of tokes of the bong would get him in the zone.

I never in my life seen someone type on a computer so fast, and without looking at the keyboard, I was astounded. The first two papers he breezed through, only time he took a breather was when it was time to inhale and exhale the bud being passed. After about the third paper, Tony jokingly words kept him comfortable with continuing to work cause honestly, he didn't have to. It was a lot of work, a lot of typing. The more and more we smoked, I was hoping he didn't get too high where he could not finish typing these papers for me, I only had until the next day. The last hit of that bong did it, after completing eight out of 10 papers in under a couple of hours, he had cut more than enough time for me to be able to complete the rest and turn in the next day. I didn't go to sleep, what took him a couple of hours took me a couple of hours, and I only had two more papers to type, both four pages apiece. Did I finish?

CHAPTER 18

SCHOLARSHIP

Hecky yeah, I finished. I gave a call to Coach S the next day and told him I made it happen. Turning in that assignment the next day gave me a sense of relief, I had taken my finals in my other classes and was set to hit the field next season. Summer school class was just an addition for me playing it safe, credits-wise. I took a bowling class. I had more than enough credits, sitting at 28 credit hours, and at the end of the semester, I was no longer on probation, academic-wise. During that summer, I was invited to participate in conditioning with the team. A year away from football, I was quite rusty and most definitely out of shape. A Challenge was always thrown my way, and this challenge was me being strong enough to build the confidence that I had as a high school superstar football player. On the field, I was still classified as a freshman, and a sophomore, weird. A handful of guys knew who I was, but I was just a freshman for the most part to the upper-class. The expectation for me was set high, not just me setting them, but coaches as well. During seven on seven, I was thrown out there at cornerback, a position I used to, straight lockdown. Sheesh, I remember stepping up online with DH, and off the line, I swear, I was hip to hip with him. The seasonal wide receiver hit me with a veteran move so crucial that brought separation between us by more than 10 yards, it was a heck of a move. Luckily Coaches never attended seven on seven's cause that might have lowered the expectation of my ability. It didn't strip me from my confidence, more of, step your game up player, type feeling. You best to believe I did. As the first game of the season was approaching, I was now participating in the team workouts and conditioning, the muscle memory that I thought was lost began developing into a collegiate-level football player. Eight weeks before we face off against our first opponent was approaching fast. All the incoming freshman and three prop 48 players were bought in a week or two ahead of the upperclassmen. This time with just the freshman and prop 48 was pretty much evaluation for where we were at skill and ability-wise. This is what I did, all I had to do, was performed, and that I did. For the coaches, this period of evaluating who could compete at the collegiate level was studied closely. I was an all-around athlete, and my athleticism allowed me to stand out. I will be honest, I thought I could play corner, but coaches saw me as a Free Safety.

For all my incoming freshman, high school seniors, even juniors, let's just say athletes consider playing at the next level. Get ready and stay prepared because you will receive a playbook the size of a textbook. The muscle memory that I had built up from the academic school year properly prepared me to treat the playbook like a three hour credited class. I had to learn it, study it, and memorize it because I would soon be tested on it. About two weeks before, we had to play against South Florida, I was moved to play Free safety. I was being tested because I had little time to learn the plays to be a part of the starting unit. I'm smarter than you think. People learn what they want to learn.

The Mental preparation and physicality that is needed to come in your first season and get playing time is a whole other test. This level isn't high school, but the comparison of a high school freshman starting on varsity is the same. I'm trying to say that you must have the confidence to compete with your mentality, not being as mature as older individuals who are already seasoned. If you plan on playing your first season and being the man, you better have what it takes not to be exposed to being immature, on the field, on the court, in whatever you do, it's about you being the young bull in the situation. Visualize this for those that play football, even the ones that don't or didn't. I was 18, going on 19, still super young, missed a whole year of playing football and conditioning at a top-level, and here it is, you on the football field banging heads and shoulders with some grown-ass men. I was still in the process of becoming, while some had already become. It was more intriguing to me as an Athlete coming from where I was from because I couldn't see myself not being the best or just being weak as fuck. This mighty feeling doesn't have anything to do with Chipolar. We gone take the Chi off and say Polar, if we were talking Physics, you must be electrifying, we are talking Geometric you're probably going to be in the cosmic section, even if we are talking about Astronomy, it's a Star who emits light. The moral of it, you must be a star, be electrifying and set the tone where your light shines so bright, you be moving throughout the cosmic section.

Prime example, the heart of Allen Iverson, who led his team to that championship that year but was dealing with energy forces from another direction that was trying to stop him from emitting that kind of light. I'm talking about that Michael Jordon type of stardom that puts you in the category as some other the biggest stars because of their electrifying Merkabah that rotates 55ft in every direction, and you see their aura. Or a Kobe Bryant type of mentality to master the game and become the best version of yourself. It takes a lot for an 18, 19-year-old young man to go out on the football field and withstand the mental durability not to feel like you cannot compete. Seniors and Juniors have a couple of years on you, they have been through the program, the nics and bruises. They literally shed blood, sweat, and tears to become the best at what they did. I was taught to live by the 5p's. If you know, then you know, what understood ain't to be explained. I lived by those 5p's and still do. I recall sitting in my dorm room during camp, all alone, and I was just visualizing myself being great. Our first game was approaching a week from now, and school was also about to begin. It wasn't so much of the school I was focused on; it was me being on the field and making some big plays. When I suddenly had an anxiety attack, I will never forget. This anxiety attack was properly preparing me. I was so eager to prevent myself from having poor performances, only the greats can relate. I was in my dorm room all alone praising, Thanking God in advance about what I was about to show the world I could do as a Division 1 football player.

CHAPTER 19

SEASON

August 30, 2001, South Florida vs. NIU, the first game of the season, started at Free Safety. I didn't know what to expect, it was a different vibe than playing at Gately or Stagg Stadium. Twenty-six thousand in attendance, and before the beginning of the game, I could spot two proud parents that were in support of me. I could see the sparkle in my parent's eyes from the stadium lights. The glistening in their eyes was also the reflection of me radiating my divine light on the field. Priceless moment. I had worked hard to get to this moment, and they knew it. That extra spark from my parents meant so much to me every single game. Who would of ever thunk it? I got eligible to play college football, and for the most part, a couple of days before class begun, I was offered a full-ride scholarship. That was also a burden uplifted off of my parents. A full ride scholarship means many more incentives for student- athletes. The real incentive is getting a free education, but you have to milk the system.

In the home opener, I recorded ten tackles. Not bad for my first collegiate football career game. The heart and mentality I explained earlier in a paragraph, the spirit of greatness, was conjured minus the rituals. What they say, "it has to be in you, and not on you." That test came along in the red zone, 10-yard line. It's a 6'7, 300 pound, Seminole-looking Floridian, pulling my way on a block to lead a power 24 dive. In football, you either gone be getting hit or doing the hitting. I step up in the hole and blew it up, disrupted the whole play up. The chant from the band and the cheers, mixed with the bell ringing in my head, hearing the pow, boom, bang, spat sound sent me somewhere else. When I hit him, and the crowd adlibs with the band playing music, was playing so loud in my head, was a small, but big diagnosis of my Chipolarness, right there, I'm talking about right there, right there. At that given moment I travelled every dimension at one given time and ended up back in my body. Just last semester, I was nobody, not to prominent. I performed, but it clicked a switch on in my head while taking on that hit in the red zone with that lineman. That enticement of stardom, my name getting called on the intercom throughout the game, me working so hard in the classroom, the doubt, the hate, the unknowing, all those feelings sent radiation through my body. My confidence level went through my crown chakra.

The next day on campus, a couple of students put a name with a face after our first win. That next week on the schedule was the University of Illinois. I still hadn't come down from last week's high, so I was still charged up. Powerful prayers, humbleness, not being overzealous, gratitude to the grind, and balancing egotistical perspective was not going to turn me down. I was amped, geeked, I was locked in. This feeling was one of the most electrifying moments. The fact that I was able to sit back and appreciate all the hard work I put into getting eligible, played my first collegiate game, moving forward with progress was just me going with the flow of things. Weeks would start to fly by, so keeping that momentum was now instilled in me. Mondays and Tuesdays were the most intense practices throughout the week. This week was big. It was big because it was an in-state rivalry, and it was being televised on Channel 7 and ESPN+. Many players like myself once probably thought or had hopes of playing for the Fighting Illini, and for whatever reason, it got narrowed down, and NIU took a chance on them. If that's not the case, not saying we weren't good enough, but we belong, where we belonged, at that given time, especially if it's divine. Our team was locked in. Even if any player wanted to play for them, I guaranteed you didn't want to play against us. We were some dawgs. One thing I notice is that all my teammates had some sort of unbalanced polarity. Those with unbalance polarity poles released their symptoms during game time. It was this sort of craziness, not too far from how I was brought up when it was time to whoop some ass. We weren't getting our ass beat no matter who you were. If you were to win, we lost with class and gained respect from any opponent.

On September 8, our game was getting many press conferences, as we were being hosted by the Fighting Illini and a crowd of 45,000 fans. All week we prepared as we prepared for any team, although this was only my second collegiate level football game, the level of focuses was competing, competing at the highest level that they thought we were not on. Not trying to be arrogant or overzealous, we never showed a sign of fear, and honestly, I never felt like that when I competed on any level of sports. Unless it was just something I hadn't masted yet, like ping pong or golfing, preferably what I'm familiar with, speaking in a term like hooping, football, baseball, and even track, I'm not saying I was the fastest, but I can throw that in there.

NIU wasn't known for having a winning program in the previous years, but 2001 was the beginning of a program over, like a makeover, get it, a program over. Whatever. You know where the program turns around for the better. Taking on that field in Champaign, Illinois, is a game I am looking for to this day. If it was up there, it would be stuck there, but for the ones that know, know. Ok, they will argue about who won, and you right, we lost 17-12. But when I tell you, they were not expecting us to come out and play smash-mouth football. They did not know what was hitting them. NIU huskies was not no pushover, I could only imagine, coming from our opponents. Even though they didn't take a chance on me, I was glad to play against them. I didn't know about all the worldwide media coverage this game would get. I told you what channel it was on, but I didn't know whom it would touch and see it.

Like my entire hometown, and I know it was two instate names, but I was just into playing some ball. I had no idea, me knocking off the quarterback's helmet would get millions of views way before IG was popping. The fact I was in the NFL mentality and thought a quick celebration of me upping two twin imaginary Glocks like I was in the Wild Wild West was not your typical celebration. I could have foot worked, I could have done anything that didn't symbolize the portraying of the things I was possibly attached too, due to my past. It was war, especially when you have 5 Big 300+ lineman trying to hem you up for taking off their quarterback helmet. From kickoff, they thought we were some punks, but they knew from the blow of the whistle, we were going to be a problem.

We never showed any fear, although we were the underdogs, best believed it, we gave whomever a run for their money. My 17 tackles recorded weren't enough to stop the 17-12 points outcome lost. A 5-point difference was still shocking to the bookies, I bet. What was more shocking too is that I had a big write up in the Chicago Sun-times, from the head coach stating I should be suspended for knocking off the quarterback helmet because he was sliding, and if we were the NFL, I would get fined $25,000 for spearing, they called it. I call it hard nose football. It was a good game; I think it was more of us showing up and showing out. We took that one on the chin, people were expecting a knockout. On a positive note, I received player of the week award for my first time, in only my second college game. National notoriety began to take notice. For many, this starts to feed the ego, for me, it was food for my soul because being on the righteous path felt promising.

In the same way, that notoriety was getting me all the recognition a student-athlete could dream of off rip. Despite doing my thing on the field, a cutie pie I had my eyes on, didn't care too much for football shit, she wasn't jocking it. That Monday, the school newspaper had a big article on the front page of it. I'm wondering why when I hit campus, everybody and they mama speaking to me. My nickname was boogie, girls ain't never said nothing to me, "hey Boogie."

Now I know I am a cool-ass person, and I don't be letting shit get to my head, but I see how some people get caught up in being overzealous or egotistical, I was showing gratitude. People I didn't even know, talking about replays as if we were watching a film and studying the last game. I got back to my dorm, Lincoln Hall, and I swear I was the man, I'm all on the front of the newspaper. Be humble, my friend, be humble, and don't be to thirsty, just because you the man doesn't mean every woman will be into you. Facts. On the front of the newspaper and all, I see it in her hand, push up on her, and she still played me. Honestly, I don't even know if she was paying attention to the article because she was in the middle of the newspaper. I shot my shot. It didn't hit though; I was fresh and all. But no good. She wasn't going. At All. She gave me convo, though, even her name. Now, this is where that Chipolar shit kicked in. She was super dope. Some say thirsty, some say, stalker, crazy, tripped, or I liked her. By you being a student, we all had emails that were assigned to us. I was able to look up her information, inviting her to hang out. I got a response.

The reply was "no." But, at least she entertained, showed some type of attention. It was enough to give me some type of hope. She was gorgeous, from the hood, same place, Englewood. She attended a more prestigious high school, so her hoodness mix with class, I felt it was something to pursue. Regarding me trying to connect with my college sweetheart, I wasn't hard upon a woman. I was a student-athlete. Perks and incentives, parties, and kickbacks were off the meter.

CHAPTER 20

GAMBLING

Meanwhile, that week we had a bye week, and I had to skip the partying for the weekend and hopped on I-88 headed back home, it was a one-day trip. When I touched down on the land, it was shocking to those who just saw me holding a press conference on ESPN. At this time, the conscious mind frame I had worked to get to a level of discipline on campus was slightly broken. Not everyone was hipped to me playing college ball, especially the ops I had made along the way, growing up. Everyone knows bullets have no names. Was this 24hr trip home worth everything I worked so hard for? So many student-athletes have lost their lives with a simple trip back home.

The time I was there was nearly enough to kiss Mom's dukes on the cheek, kick the bobos with my pops, probably pull up on my ex, and holler at a couple of the guys. I snuck home, no one knew, I had hooked with my homie Tay Tay. We were in motion to make a couple of rounds holler at my people, and Whoop Whoop, police sirens. The damn Slick boys. Unmarked vehicle. Man, they hopped out so quickly, before we know it, they had us stretch out like rubber bands. Come to find out, we were riding his cousin's car, who lived in Minnesota but had a warrant in Chicago. What I know now, them dickheads broke all types of laws. No one was ever harmed, and we were profiled, never broke the law. They tore the steering wheel up, looking for drugs, the door panels ripped off the interior of the door. The most intriguing part of the whole situation, they didn't find anything, and when they sent us about our way, we were left to assemble all parts destroyed. Just say if we were riding dirty, the whole career, down the drain. I told bro to drop me off at my parent's home, surprise them, and Mom surprised me with a good ole home-cooked meal. This when I was eating pork, some fried pork chops, some cabbage, sweet potatoes, and cornbread. Thank God I was able to kiss moms on the cheek and kick it with my pops, if the police had slammed me for jaywalking, my parents, coaches, and teammates would have been let down. Early A.M, I was headed back to DeKalb.

The whole ride back home was sort of like a reflection over my life that constantly got replayed in my head. These replays were the 24hr journey that just took place at a place I was so profoundly rooted too. Besides me heading down south every other summer or some other miscellaneous instate demographical location, I was far enough away from what had significant stipulations on my way of decision making. Far enough to be removed from having to worry about my ops or the local cops and slick boys, who didn't want to see me win. Being away from home for some time, I became accustomed to a new atmosphere with less of those worries of becoming a statistic. Not saying I couldn't, cause ideally, I was way out of my boundary, I felt like, especially me, being enrolled in someone's university. This reflection allowed me to appreciate the growth I was enduring. Mainly where I was from and where I was headed back to. I had something to look forward to. First time I have ever been excited for Monday class on top of a game that upcoming weekend. Me making the right decisions started to become more beneficial on my end relative to my football career and grades. Another adversary moment could have put me back in a funk when I got back on campus from the short trip home. I was back with a more sense of purpose.

Getting into the flow of things became second nature to me with the mandatory study table Tuesday through Friday for those assigned to. If you missed, well consequence, would be 6 am workout, and isn't no telling what that consists of. The last thing I was trying to miss is a study table session. I got additional help on an assignment. They assigned me to a tutor. I know many people think or even ask me; did I ever have to do my college work? Damn skippy, I did my college work. Now, don't get me wrong, I wasn't the smartest, and often I would recognize my strength and my weakness when it came to education, all I could do is try. The luxury of some jocks not having to do work or finding that smart chick to do your work, I only seen in movies. I have heard stories, mainly at big-time colleges, of an athlete who didn't have to go to class, but that's rare, and he must know he is going straight to the league. As I thought, I was going to be the first high school football player to go straight to the NFL. School? School what? You couldn't tell me shit about school. You can be the coldest athlete, but if you are not getting the grades, you just going to be an athlete with aspirations. I was gradually becoming a student. I was maturing, this also showed on the field. Balancing all aspects of college, normalcy, was a feeling I would get so often. I think any college is like an Atlanta party lifestyle. In Atlanta, it's a party Sunday through Sunday. Clubs go up on a Tuesday, that's a song that can get played on a Tuesday in the club, and the club nine times out of 10 is going up. Imagine all the young college adults that go to college in Atlanta, and where they go hang out, they hang out. I don't know that might too much partying, but you get the logistics, if you get caught up in the party scene, you aren't going to get nothing accomplished because it's a party Sunday to Sunday. Most of the time, during the season, we would hit a club after the game or you were trying to score on a little baddy. For the most part, from Sunday to Sunday, if it wasn't study table or preparing for our next opponent, anything was up in the air. Endless opportunities when you are networking with the right people. That's one thing I did, I made sure I plugged.

Yea, I was a student-athlete, but some of the best resources on campus, was just students, if not students, the locals had connections. I invariably implored myself to attack righteous endeavors. Enough begging to the Universe will have things manifesting rapidly. With my name ringing bells around campus, me reaching a different demographic of the campus was offered with a radio station. Typical path set forth for the Athlete life in the sports world. I get it now.

Most of every Ex-athlete starts his career in the sports world and ends off in the sports broadcasting world. At least some form of Sports Entertainment. Two of the homies and I stumbled across an opportunity to host our own radio show. Why did they do that? Things were starting to get interesting now. After auditioning for a slot, we were penciled in three times a week. Balancing this task and practice, study table, and personal life gave me an outlet to exercise my First Amendment. I don't think you guys understand the power behind having access to a microphone. This access was granted. Intro went something like this, the name of our show was called "The Block." So, "what's up, good people? You are now tuned into Northern Star Radio, that was a sweep prerecorded to introduce us. Then we would come on, with a dope ass introduction beat, "you are now tuned in to "The Block," this yo boy Boogie, this yo boy Sonny, and your one and only Drezz, and we out her posted on "The block, serving you some dope ass music along with some good ass intriguing topics, blah blah. Shit was super dope, but as I think of now, a little unsafe and unwanted attention from those not liking you exercising your rights. You thought I was exercising because I played ball, just imagining me not knowing about exercising my rights but having no filter with what came out of my mouth at the time. After all, I was straight off the block. Not the radio station I created, but the blocks of the South Suburbs and the city of Chicago sides, mainly Southside. With me being in the Radio station, or even playing ball and in the field, realistically coming from those two metaphors, my mentality, the way I moved, what I did when no one was looking had to be utilized even being in college. The reason being, my Chipolarness was getting fed.

We were eating well on the field; we had defeated Sam Houston state that following weekend. That game was a breeze, it kicked off with a trickery play that had us on our toes in the first quarter, from there, it was a wrap, blew them boys, off the field. Northern, for some odd years, the football program didn't have much impact on the campus. Now 2-1, for the first time in history, things began to start looking on the up and up. With Toledo been our MAC rivalry, we were up for a challenge in our next game. Preparation was something you had to prepare for if you get the drift. As a student-athlete, the level of discipline required more energy than it did for me as a prop 48, my freshman year. Focusing on just school and getting eligible for the next year, mixed with a little bit of kicking it, is much easier than being locked in on five or six things at one time. Remember the old saying, you have to be able to chew gum and walk? I felt like I was being challenged with chewing gum and walking across a tight rope with a blindfold. There is a price with being the man. Only four games in, I started paying the price. Being a student for me now had become second nature. The challenge for me was performing at the top level every game day. My name all in the newspaper, I have become an in-house name. Although I had one of the coolest names in college football, my name had always rung bells back home.

I was often reminded by people that knew me growing up as a shorty in the hood. I had a run into one of the guys from back home that knew me as the old guy I used to be. Fam probably hadn't seen me since the 8th grade or just floating through the hood my teen years. Still, one of my best homies to this day, seen me and was in shock that I was even in school. All he was saying was, "man, are you serious" with the facial expression of Awe naw. I was representing some of the guys, that did get guided in the right aspect of our knowledge, which was education. Learning how to adjust in society without being a menace began that day. In other words, learning how to be a student, and not just an athlete reminded me, some people see me as something else than an athlete. I'm about toot my horn again, if I didn't already, I was a Superstar.

CHAPTER 21

ADVERSARY

Toledo University was on the schedule that 29th of September. We hit the road to face off the Rockets. They were our rivalry. This was one team that defeated us almost in all previous years. While watching the film on the rockets throughout the week, they were a conservative team. A team with a consistent flow throughout the game, with a mixture of screens. We are known for flying to the ball, so we planned to see it before it happens, then react. The pace of college football is a fast pace and intense. It's not a play that you can take off. We were finally looking like a team that could defeat the rockets, finally. The first couple of quarters, it wasn't not taking off from them. They were trying to put the ball in the air, but we managed to keep it on the ground. "Huskies for the stop." It was some hard-nose football going on that Saturday. It wasn't a game that I played so far that didn't require all my football powers.

I activated my football senses, tackle after tackle, I was trying to bring the thunder. It's like I put a special code in, back back, towards A, Nintendo style. Next play, interception, snagged my first one. Hit my first defender, bap, bap, chopped him down, like I was Peter Warwick, got hit by the next defender, trying to take out my legs, he clipped me a little bit. I got my feet right, tight rope the sideline, and took it to the house, a pick for 6. The second hit I took on my knee would give me my first college football injury.

I had so much adrenaline pumping, I had no idea because I finished the game. They ran the score up, and we took an L. My right knee had swollen up like a chicken injected with steroids, I was in inscrutable pain. The first time this city boy dipped. Dip, I'm not talking about, ran, no dip baby dip shit. That country dip, well I wouldn't say country dip, I want to say the dip that the dippers be doing, my granddaddy uses to dip. But I grabbed a big glob of that dip from one of the White boys on the bus headed back home, and laid out in the middle of the bus in some of the most unbearable pain I ever experienced. If I could have smoked a blunt, I would flame it up, dead smack on the back of the bus, to relieve the pain radiating in my knee in that one spot. Honestly, I couldn't wait to smoke a blunt, I see this required a different special code I had put in to perform. The only thing this wasn't a video game, and in real life, this injured player was out for the next 4-6 weeks. If it weren't for that tobacco dip I put in my mouth, I wouldn't have made that 4hr ride back. I had to see the trainer the next day, where x-rays and an MRI had to be taken. A torn meniscus (MCL). That little flame I had lit died out; I was firing up every blunt I could with the light I did have. Discourage, lost, hurt, confused, why me? Why did I have to sustain an injury that would set me back 4-6 weeks from showcasing my talent.

I was out there balling balling, not crying, but doing my thang. And I was now feeling like I was feeling my freshman year as a prop 48, but worst. I couldn't run, jump, move laterally, hit a dance move or nothing. I was down down. The next couple of weeks would require some intense rehabilitation, 6 am and during practice hours. If I want to bounce back more vigorously than ever, I had to commit myself to rehab every chance I got. I had some support along the way, it was cool being told I was going to be ok, but no one knew what I was experiencing as a person. Adversary at its finest, that's when I can honestly say I learned a new word. Adversary, adversaries, was something I always experience but would name it hard times or bad times, heck, even bad karma would be the name, if shit wasn't going in your favor. Here it is. I go from being on Espn, Newspapers, your child's favorite football player too, Where's Lionel? Rehab, class, radio station, and at the crib blazing a fat one with my lady friend, where I would be. I was determined to get back; wasn't no way I wasn't going to come back stronger than ever. I had got pain relief often by going to the radio station and doing my radio show. It was something about being able to speak on the air. I would often get asked about my football status, but I quickly separated those two characters for my sanity. I didn't want to make it a, what would we say now, a football podcast. I wanted to have the WGCI or Power 92.3

feeling, and we did just that. The concern of whether I was ok wasn't such a concern after the second week or two. The team had to continue without my electrifying energy, and I supported from the sideline fully. Coaches and players could see the hurt in my eyes.

Weeks were going by, and I was at about 80 percent, I was starting to get most of my forward and lateral movement back. I was doing well in my classes because I felt like I had more time to lock in on my studies. Over-focused on my rehabbing and my classes, I discovered I was smarter than I thought and stronger too. Within four weeks, I pushed myself back on the field in time to play Eastern Michigan. First game back, we won, I played slightly timid, next game Ball State, ten tackles one pick for 6, also received player of the game. Last game of the season, we faced off against Wake Forrest, an ACC opponent, Wake Forrest was also our first opponent for the following season. We lost to them 35-38 on their home turf. Us playing them the last game of the season would also be a continuance of the previous game, we knew what to expect. Too lose by three-point to An ACC team gave us some confidence about facing them next year. I always felt we could beat any team we played.

Off-Season got more intense as things died down around the stadium. Besides working out at a set time or indulging in some filming on-campus was another recreational thing to keep me active. I kept myself busy with the radio station coming up with creative ideas to get it rocking and rolling. Marketing schemes were implemented to fill that void of not being in season. Newspaper ads with the block boys promoting their show bought extra attention on top of us being student-athletes. Man was it some extra perks with being a student- athlete, not just an ordinary athlete, but a fake superstar at that, mix with some gangster, and later discovering my nerdiness, through being a player, I would consider myself all-around solid. Better yet Intune. I was shown a lot of Love, I also showed Love, but you always have your haters. Most of the time, you would put yourself in the line of hate by showing up to a party on campus. I wouldn't even say it was hating, more of some young college students having some drinks, getting scummy by the end of the night the alcohol did just what it was supposed to do, get someone out their body. Spirits that activated their vessel, gave the person courage as if they can beat up anyone at any given time. That is not the case. More like, they drunk as fuck, did some dumb shit, and his homie got his ass whooped, intermingled in with too much testosterone. Mostly just being on some tough shit mixed with the alcohol would be the first stir up to the hate. I never cared too much for the drunks or the ones who got out of their bodies. Knowingly, how people were when they got stupid drunk often gave me a sensibility on how the night would go if someone were to step on the wrong person's shoes or try to holler at the wrong dude, girl. In addition, too, it's the stereotype of football players always on some tough shit. In many of my conflicts on campus involving fistfights felt more gang-related than just an ordinary all-out brawl.

CHAPTER 22

AVERAGE JOE WHO?

At any given time, I'm moving around on a party night, I am with athletes, at least 20 of my football partners. On top, about 5 of the guys from around the land would often come to kick it. Real recognize real, I locked in with some non-athletes who learned some of the ways of life as myself and others. The frats had their Chiefs and Indians. You even had real street cats. It was often a night mixed with a lot of fuckery, going on if you wanted to be a part of that life. I always felt like it was too many fines ass, women, out and about to be hooting and hollering on some tough shit, but most of the time, the reason for getting so loud was to let the girls think you were no hoe, A.K.A, you were about to fuck something up. Things would often go down on campus that wasn't far off from feeling like you back in the hood. Internally, I was changing; I was adapting.

I wouldn't say so much of changing cause sometimes gangsta shit would come out of me. I had had a couple of conflicting situations during my first semesters, but never any hands or feet thrown. Off-season granted us too much time to kick it and get involved in real-life campus life. At this time, my second semester, I was living in the low-key dorm, I would call it. I branched off to Neptune after a temporary stay in Lincoln. Neptune is where all the students who had high IQ's I would say, and weren't into the campus things, would often live.

Being under the radar for me was a mind-frame developed in the streets as a youngin and is often a skill picked up due to boss like activities. Something instilled from day 1. As I stated before, sometimes on campus felt like being on an active block out south somewhere in Englewood. You had your fake tough guys, we called them toll booth gangsters. When they rolled in town, paid their toll, they felt like they had a pass to do gangster shit in a small ass corn town. Don't get it twisted, most did come from that lifestyle, but it would be safe to say most wanted to better their lives. If they did get on gangsta time, it was just in them. It was definitely in me, I was finding balance, a couple of times, I was knocked off balance. What's that saying? It has to be in you, not on you? So, if I ever expressed it, that's what's was inside of me, it's because it was at that time, not all the way out of my system, so if I ever got tested, it was bought out of me. I did what I was supposed to do on the field, but off the field, I was a different person.

A Radio personality, student-athlete, someone who was plugged, now experiencing all walks of life, and a developed discipline from what some would call an aspect of hard knocked life, I knew of my superpowers somewhat. One of their superpowers was, I hated losing. I wanted to see everyone win, except my opposition. At the time, I didn't have any, but for sure found some. Well, the homie stumbled up on some.

We were both from the same place. Attending high school together created a different bond automatically, then some of my college friendships. My boy Nate was the man on the hooping side, going to Robeson together and both having the same out view on we were from, and where we were headed, we also had the same outlook when it came to what we stood for, our integrity and dignity was always highly represented. Our knowledge and understanding pushed us to be great. But let's be honest, because this shit is quite interesting to have someone like me give you this story because Chipolar is a great definitional word to explain some of the Chicagoan's characterizations if you have ever been trying to put the finger on what it is about Chicago people. We know when to click it on and click it off. I will be the first one to tell you, ain't shit wrong with us. We know exactly what the heck is going on. A lot of the time, we Chicago people get a bad rep just for saying we from there, but the true person who is either from there or has honestly spent some time there or with someone who has Chipolar is scratching their head trying to figure out why we some of the coolest people in the world. But good God almighty, if you push that button shit can get ugly, that Chipolar start kicking in, and all the medicine is, is love and respect. If you weren't trying to show

Love or ain't trying to get Love, I think that's when the problem occurs. We just are quick to solve it. My freshman year incident with the young lady, whom I hadn't apologized to for hocking on, fake new boyfriend and my homie had words in front of one of the dormitories. Already having some friction from the freshman year incident of my hocking on a chick would ignite the situation. The dude felt some type of way when I walked to greet my homie. We not even going to associate Chipolar with this instance because it is not that some people might not have it all, we just know how to take it there. A couple of words was exchanged, and all I could remember was hands and feets. Buddy was shaking like a tail feather. Hoping in our 1986 white cutlass, you would have thought we were in the hood, how I'm explaining it. I had my Buck 150 on my head, shit happen quickly, 3 min later, we were in my Neptune dorm room, standing on what we had believed in, Aiding and assisting. If I could name this next little part of the book, its name would be "Campus Wars."

CHAPTER 23

CAMPUS WARS

If we were to describe this war, one describable word is "all-out." It is subliminally happening amongst us, Americans vs. Africans. This part of my story is not to cause any confusion. The war among Americans and Africans is another book within itself. I can't say I am from Africa. After extensive research discovering my family was indigenous to American land, I would just say we were not from the same tribe. Although they went to school in Chicago and were probably from one of the sides of town, they stress that they were indigenous to Nigeria. From a broader perspective, it was brothers fighting brothers. After the 3 minutes had passed up within the next 10 minutes, about 10 African brothers were ready to seek revenge.

Pull up game was strong even in the early 2000s, all with the chirp of a Nextel. It was no iPhones, wasn't any dropping your location. Known for scamming and all the trickery shit, African buddy tracks me and bro-down, asap. Someone had to give up my location. I stayed on the first floor, I looked outside my window, and they were super deep. Remember, it was only two of us. They fake had us boxed in, but come on now, even way in the cornfields, we were plugged but wasn't any going outside until our guys pulled up, and they were pulling up, pulling up. So, when they pulled up, about six of our guys pulled up and just posted up. I could have called about another ten people, but soldiers were kept for another day. Was no keeping us cooped up in the room like some bitches; walked outside the dorm, and they ain't keep the same energy. We pretty much talked about why we knocked his homie out and what the problem was right there on site.

Furthermore, buddy and his peoples kept it cool, but it was on from there. The shit began to get out of hand, just feet and hands, luckily no guns. I was taught to Aid and Assist your brother in any righteous endeavors. The loyalty that lies in the streets and those you love dearly is something most Chicagoans learn early on. Off the strength and principles, if you were in my circle, was no second-guessing if I was going to ride.

I needed to be focus on my damn schoolwork out there fighting. Tripping, that's what I was doing. The habits I was repeating were already learned and weren't apart of any syllabuses. The conflict that played out between the Africans and us was weird. It would never get sent up during class hours if we saw one another on campus, only taking place at a club or an after-hours event. Straight Chipolar shit, since we were in our off-season, fighting every weekend was like a recreational sport. But these ops weren't playing fair. A week or two after that first incident, the next two events would make us undefeated, being 3-0. In the second brawl, they showed up a couple of men short and couldn't cover the whole field. They always managed to try and catch us late night coming out of the club, this was when I knew I was the solution and they were the problem, because that same 2nd fight night, they call themselves alerting one of my homies that they were waiting on me to get out and wanted holler at me. My homie feeling the low vibrational energy, instantly took the position. The dude wanted his lick back. You will often hear some of the guys from Chicago tell a story about legend fights. One of the key phrases they will elaborate on is how 3 or 4 of us will take on 7 or 8, even more, guys and probably whoop their ass. But on the flip side, 7 to 8 of us beating on three guys ain't fair, they are getting stumped out, and that just what happened that night. They were outnumbered. You can't stand a chance with some in shape college athletes, most of them from the hood and with the shits. One punch led to someone getting their face kicked like a soccer-style scholarship field goal kicker hitting a game-winner —no Ray Finkle.

It was just a big ole cluster fuck, it was like four on 8. Me the champ, one of them and the challenger, one who got put to sleep from the first dispute. He was trying to redeem himself, he didn't have a chance, I dropped him like a three-credit-hour class. That Monday A.M., I was sitting in the dean's office facing my consequences. They then went to go snitch on your boy. I guess the beating was so bad, it's no way the guy that got his face kicked off, could look himself in the mirror. I found myself twiddling my fingers sitting at the desk of the dean who had my scholarship in his hand, ready to revoke it. For one, I never admitted to fighting, it was just still an assumption. It was so much of a big deal, but they had no proof, I had knocked this dude out twice. He wouldn't even want to big me up like that at the time, but I foresaw he let the dean know in this instance, because I was giving him the flux. Instead of getting everything I worked hard snatch in a blink of an eye, I was placed on three year's probation. You see, the irony of the probation was to keep me skating on thin ice, I was even giving community service to do. The community service was one of the best things I had been assigned, and I had to complete. My community service consisted of me reporting to Coach O's house. Who is Coach O? I don't know if I mentioned him early on in my college career, but at one point, he was my bowling teacher, in my summer school session the freshman year, I was struggling to get eligible. Fortunately, me being assigned to do community service work with him, I began to gain so much wisdom along the rest of my journey as a student- athlete. Fun Factor: Coach O was one of the first Indigenuos to play in the professional Negro League.

Some of the great Athletes are giving mentors, or God sends someone along your path to guide you in the right direction, it's up to you to take that into heed. This was a clear sign given to me that someone willing to share that space of greatness with me. Being a household name on campus and

Coach O and the dean being good friends, he might have come up with a way to save me because he saw something in me. Every weekend I would find myself after hours of cutting grass and doing lawn work, going through archives of legendary pictures and other memorabilia of people like Jackie Robinson, Hank Aarons, all types of classic things that often came with stories that should be in history books. Coach O was like my grand pops. He also had a son that played Profession Football for the San Diego Chargers for a while, his conversation and picture showing became inspirational for me, I was starting to mature through the guidance of Coach O. He would elaborate on talks about me amongst the people that were football crazy for NIU. Many times, I was the topic of the conversation because of the hard nose football I played, and my determination to being great was not under shown. Mentor-like, talks of me being a future professional football player were given out of inattention to do what's right at the time for me to stay out of the office of my Coaches and the dean as well. I was on the verge of being kicked out one more incident. Shownuff, next week, after taking this matter to our coaches and even the athletic director, it was another brawl, this time involved in over 200 people. I know, right, Sheesh. Two hundred people, fam, they came with their whole tribe.

So, we thought everything was in the clear after being ratted on to our coaches and athletic director. We decided to throw a party on a Thursday night. I forget the name of the spot. This party was one of the most epic parties ever on campus. I'm talking about ladies everywhere, people dancing, good drank, and even high five's a couple of times as if a good play was made. You know I was doing my two-step; we were in that joint boogieing. By the time i was about to start footworking working, the party had spilled to outside, in a split of a second. Shit, it happens so fast. All- out brawl. Like that day like that day they pulled up on me at the dorm, they pulled up to the club—this time with a whole team, no exaggeration, about a 30 of their Nigerian homies. No cap, I think they might of flew some of them straight from the Motherland, still dress in the authentic garments made from scratch from one of their Queens. The only thing them boys didn't come with were some spears. The way they kicked it off was so Americanized though, and something a thug would have straight did, even a racist, but you should visualize a racist at a bar pulling this. It's a movie scenario.

The beer bottle already cracked on the concrete surface to make a sharp object created to slice and dice your ass to pieces. The first person that stepped out, which name I will keep confidential, was buck 50'd, real quick. Ignorance at its finest, especially for the 50 guys enrolled to get a degree. This was beyond major, a minor uneducated decision led to this. Not even saying this for no hee hee or no, haha's, only to give you a visualization of what happened to the homie. Remember the Martin episode with Tommy Hitman Hearns? Yea, that part. That's only because of the foolish decision to go out there by himself, and until someone stormed in the building saying he was getting jumped, isn't no telling what really could have happened to him, with the numbers being enormous, recognizing who could get these hands had to be strategically thrown. Stick and move, stick and move. The Instinct of one of the best top Free safeties in college football only enhanced the athleticism punches that were being thrown. I was being exonerated for it, any who. Got to stick and move, when dealing with a brawl that involves a mass number of people, can't be the one getting stomped out. Good thing I had that vision. I look out my peripheral, and what do we have here? The defeated challenger just won't give in until he gets his lick back, but with the footwork of a House of Matic members and a mean punch like Mike Tyson, I dropped him again like a 3-hr. class I would take another semester. Sheesh, I know he hated that cause I hated it for him, my defense is impeccable like Mayweather, what can I say.

CHAPTER 24

DETERMINATION

I got little, small, peeeeewn, but before I could make it back inside the club, a loud rev of a 1998 cutlass heads my way full steam. All I hear is the words "Imma kill you" shouted loud with my name at the end. If the cars were the Offensive line, I would say we did a 23 dive, the hole was wide open. Ran back to the club to grab my Averix jacket, it was brand new. Slipped out the side door, hit a slight jog, and took it to the house. Hopefully, this was the end zone. It was like NIU football, my years 2001-2004 playing against Toledo, we stood a chance but never won, and it always mattered about a split of a second. In minutes, a couple of the guys was beating the door down regarding what happened to the fam that got pulled into the fire first. He was on his way to get stitched up at the local University Hospital, but he claims he was good. At this point, I was already all-in. Seeking revenge on his behalf would have to be ok'd on his consent. Selfishly to say, I was 3-0, all with TKOs. On the flip side, I was on three years' probation, walking on pins and needles, one more incident, they were snatching my scholarship. One of the biggest brawls on campus I could recall. Since they caught one of our guys and did him bogus, the word did get out. I was one of the ones to send it up at the party the other night, I was in the clear with coaches and the dean. They might have sought some help for me because I had pushed it beyond all measures of turning a sweet opportunity sour. Chipolar, it just all makes sense to me, when I came up with this title or name, it's a way to describe most Chicagoans who have been fully diagnosed and put in a mind-frame of rage from day 1. The mental image perception of someone who tries to picture a Chi town state of mind, Chipolar will be the term. Well, the good and bad. Everything is not all bad. I don't refer to Chicago as Chiraq, but when you describe the war in Chicago, its comparison to war amongst the foot soldiers could be portrayed as Iraq vs U.S. cause it's never-ending. Why would this title line up with a story like this? Although this happens around many college campuses, some stories even led to someone getting killed in some instances. Do you think NIU was off the chain? Imagine SIU, a long way from Chicago, but you know how many people migrate there and intertwine with the people from all over, and it becomes a Chicago against everybody? Even if the Chicago person is in the right, you are about to witness their Chipolar kick in full access, but Monday Am sitting in class trying to be great or at the library trying to finish up a paper due the next day.

Can't we just be great? But I understand we are multi-universal beings living in the same world. Oh yeah, and the

Media controls everything—side note. Coaches knew where I was coming from, what type of area they were recruiting from in Chicago. Granted, they did take a chance, but I was talented; they couldn't take that away from me. Knucklehead, you couldn't just tell off rip, I wasn't molded like that. Not to be loud and boastful, most Chicagoans aren't. So, what you will get from us is a solid, loyal, loving, caring person, unless that other side is trigger by some type of goofy shit that we feel is bogus. Now you are imagining this story I'm telling, it's like, wtf. The little children that see that side won't be able to picture it until now, and they are up in age. In the same world, I was attending sports events and signing autographs, press conferences, I was doing community events, in other words, righteousness. Just imagine if they exposed the side of me terrorizing someone that thought they could terrorize me. I would do what I need to do to protect that image. I wasn't just a thug or a hoodlum, as they would say, I was an honorable person striving to do what was right, play some ball, and get some education. I wasn't trying to hurt anybody. At this point, I was just a target. That comes with being the man, someone will always have it for you. Let's speak from a spiritual aspect, laws of the Universe, karma to be specific. After having 3 TKO'S under my belt, even being in the right, my opponent didn't have to lift a finger for me to be injured or hurt, or even for the most part, feel his pain.

Next season was approaching, and I was getting noticed for having an outstanding season finishing with 96 tackles, four interceptions with two touchdowns, playing just 8 out of 12 games. Wake Forest was first on our schedule. They were also the last team we had played last season and lost to them on their home turf. This time they had to come to Brigham Field at Huskies Stadium, a tough place to play in front of 31,000, although the stadium holds the same amount, it's not a comparison to at least 15,000 of those fans having Chipolar, and they rooting for us. Husky crazy. August 29th, 2002, Wake Forest football vs Northern Illinois Football, Huskies Stadium, kick-off 6:30 pm. Coming into this season ranked as the #9 defensive back unit in college football shows the level of talent, we produced at NIU, and the list goes on. I was hyped for this game, as I hadsome significant people to watch me showcase my talent.

My high school coach, Coach C, was there along with and Coach E. It was a big night in Dekalb, Illinois, having Wake Forest in huskie's country. In Dekalb, back in those years, it was lit, off the chain. Campus life was like no other with a winning football team finally after a long losing streak in the past. The fraternities and Soros, even the locals, had the campus. The great performance that we put on from the previous season attracted much attention nationally and locally. Honestly, now that I type about it, I was in my glow that day. Don't get it misconstrued, I played with passion, but most of the time, after a good play, the street mentality was intertwined into my celebrations or my style of play. Intimidation, a great way to put it, if you can intimidate the right opponent, the battle will be a walk in the park. In war, if you can utilize the scare tactic, your opponent will be defeated before the game even start.

Usually dealing with this type of energy rather it's sport wise or chess life decision making moves. The over aggressively one sometimes loses due to the improper way of using the Chi. Early on, I had mastered the anxiety feeling before going into any game. The butterflies, the inconsistent flow of the proper cosmic breathing, the racing thoughts of not performing at your highest level, all the doubts. I had killed that shit early on in my career. At this point, I felt and knew I was divine; although I knew it was room for growth, you couldn't tell me I wasn't one of the rawest football players in the world. I had a player or two I looked up too but not many of them. To compete at the highest level, there had to be some sort of belief in self to perform on the collegiate level. The bigger the school's name, the more focus and energy I put into that day of the game to ball out and have an outstanding performance. At this point, it was like riding a bike, along with bussing some wheelies, heck, even riding the bike backward, to show the mastery skills of a master. Remember not only are you preparing, but your opponent is also to as well. We were on the radar with being number 9 in the country, our Defensive back unit. We were some dawgs.

On top of that, our whole team was intact. With Wake Forest losing the coin toss and NIU receiving the ball at halftime, our defensive unit was up first. Starting of the 20-yard line, utilizing a defensive back terminology to relay a check to the cornerback and outside line back to check wheel, converting the backside of our defense to cover 2 to protect the quick screen, and me over my thirds, just in case the wideout keeps vertical, was the sign of maturity and knowing the offense plays beforehand.

Wake Forest was a sound team, not much trash talk was talked on their behalf. I wasn't the only trash talker amongst us Huskies, I think that was embedded in most of our players, that was that Chipolar kicking in. Silence is one way to pull your magic trick off, too much talking might just talk yourself out of a situation or in one. The first two downs were looking skeptical for Wake Forest, but with 3rd and just inches, the first down allowed them to pull their trick off. The 6th play of the game, sweep to their right our left, scraping to the ball at an angle pursuit just in case running back slips a couple of tackles, I would be there to save a touchdown. Getting to the ball is one of the main rules as a defensive player. I broke that rule like any rule that was set before me in life, and I choose not to obey, I hadn't thumped my pads yet, and I was trying to warm them up because I hadn't got any action my way since kick-off.

Remember number one rule, get to the ball, oh also, don't get hit, you do the hitting, every chance I got I was trying to run someone dead smack over. As the ball is nowhere near me, a wide receiver is pursuing me, and I feel him getting near out of my peripheral vision. As I am going to turn back to blow up his block, he drops down so fast, delivering a helmet to my right knee. Now any of you that can remember the movie The program, when the guy knee busted open, and he started going crazy on the field cause the pain he was experiencing was like no other. That was me, as soon as he hit my knee, I heard a pop so loud and felt a pain radiate through my knee so bad, I could feel the celebration from the guy, I kept knocking out on campus. Karma at its finest. It's like what had just happened to me was every punch I landed on that dude's face. I never punched myself, I know I have a mean punch, but my pride was hurt more than anything. As the whole stadium was quiet, you could hear every F-bomb dropped from the sidelines to the bleachers to the skybox. I couldn't imagine someone doing something to me so hurtful, I wanted to kill him, but it was only out of spite of being defeated.

I was now getting a dose of my medicine. This medicine wouldn't clear the instant Chipolarness I expressed right there on the field after tearing my ACL, MCL, PCL, and LCL. A lot of L's, right? I know, that's when I discovered all the tendons. I tore every last one of them. Man, was I fucked, fucked mentally, to a point I want to give up. I was now facing another adversary in my life. It's like all my energy had got drained, I wasn't even at square one, more like zero. It was hard for me to wrap my brain around getting hurt, I had never been injured in football. This was the type of injury not many bounces back from, I was ready to throw the towel in and head back home. That next day, contemplating packing my belongings and hanging it up, it looked like a wrap with the football.

All I could remember is calling my mom on the phone the next day or two and expressing to her the hurt and pain I was experiencing and how I was ready to give up, if I wasn't playing football. Seeing the bigger picture was drawn out for me through signs and symbols. I had to wake my dumb ass up and realize football was not going to be forever. So, I decided to smarten up. I became backpack Shawty. I was back to being an A Full-time student, just as I came.

CHAPTER 25

SQUARE 1

Educational-wise, this is when I tapped in. Slowly but shortly, I was forming into my Genius-hood. With my vocabulary not being as high as the one whom reads the webster dictionary during reading time; adversity was a word I need to go look up ASAP. The word adversary was often used in context when a prepped speech or some inspirational words were spoken to me to keep my head up. The damn word stuck to me to this day.

It only reminds me when something doesn't go in my favor, lame terms, going through a rollercoaster in your life, up and down, up and down. For most of my days now, I'm creating my own narrative, I'm on the up and up, but I do know what adversary means. At this time of my severe knee injury, my life had changed, before I was so up, I'm talking about up up. First, I was eligible to play, that's an up relative to what I went through to get on the field. Next, I became a household name, ranked nationally at number 9 in the country as a DB unit. I had my radio show, a couple of cuties pies on deck that had me in my glow. To add some other things that had me feeling myself, I wasn't no lame, and I had a couple of knockouts under my belt. You couldn't tell me anything. But you see how I felt myself and feeling like I was on top of the mountain, you couldn't tell me anything.

After undergoing an MRI and meeting with the Chicago Bears trainer, I discover that my knee would soon need to be reconstructed, all that high and mighty feeling like I couldn't be touched, because I been knocking out the same dude for the past couple weekends, leaving without a scratch, but got injured in a whole other war battle. This damn feeling felt like a team that goes 13-0 during the regular season, only to finish 13-1, losing the big one, throw the whole season out the window.

My whole season was on stand-by. Right knee, the size of a softball, protected by a customized brace that had me feeling vulnerable, and anyone had the ups on me. I was hurt and injured, feelings crushed, and all-around spiritually drained, I felt like I was at my lowest of the low. You think the guy I had a conflict with didn't feel like now he didn't have to lift a finger because I was now feeling his pain. I was feeling that shit, no lie, and I don't remember popping any pills, wasn't no 800mg ibuprofen was going to soothe this pain. I was smoking blunt after blunt, some good hydro weed most of the time, had me so high I would not feel anything until my high wore off, or I tweaked, forgetting I tore my whole knee ligaments thinking I could just move around like I use too.

Mentally it was draining, I never in my life been through anything like this besides tearing my collar bone back when I was young, but I played in that Sunday's football game. It was time to do some real soul searching. That search required tapping into my Chi. My internal energy became more dependable to me, before being appointed to the meaning of Chi in the Eastern system. Let's look at it from the philosophical point of view with the title of the book. Although I tied it to Chicago, Chi-town, or in other words, the Chi-raq, it goes hand in hand with how I, personally, see magic is used over Chicago natives. We call it the Chi, we say we from the Chi, and if you a real one, you love going to the Chi.

Now, let's look at Mother Earth, even just on a global scale, and I'm speaking from a metaphysical and spiritual standpoint. They say the earth has Chakras, which meant has a heart along with other organ mechanisms to operate the body. Everything thing in nature is a reflection, all the way too, the trees having a life— the Demographic of Chicago, A.K.A. The Chi might be the inner force of the earth Chi, but due to Man's creation of technology and many of the things that throw the Earth's magnetic poles off has caused a polarity shift within the earth. That's why everything is off balance. Now let's put the analogies together that I just interpreted and ponder on it. Shit deep and gets even deep, Chipolar.

Just off that along, whoever is reading that is wondering, what am I talking about, and might suggest, I do have

Chipolar. Right! Heck of a way to come up with a meaning pertaining to Mother Earth and Chicago's people. Growing up, going through situations, the struggle, and constant survival mode tactics, allowed me to experience having to dig deep inside internally to discovering my inner Chi and being strong enough to endure adversity. I wasn't balanced. My polarity poles were shifted, and I think most of us from Chicago is off-balanced. And when we are tapping into our inner Chi, that's when we experience harmony. Yea, we have some off-balance and not intune, but you have some Chicagoans that are Chipolar that are all the way Intune. They mastered their Chi force and balanced their polar and are electrifying people and magnify great things. While I was missing the entire 2002 season, I had to stay lit, the little flame I did have. Lit somehow, besides lighting up every blunt I could roll to deal with egotistical thoughts of not being looked at as being part of the team at the time. It was more of getting the perks and incentives that came with being on the field balling and winning. It was something about kicking it after the game, all the love being shown when being out and about. All I was getting now was, "man, just rehab, bro, everything going to be ok." "Fuck outta here," was the internal voice speaking, but with the external voice, I would respond with a gratitude response.

After beating Wake Forrest on national TV, 42 to 41, we were on the road to having a great season, I was rooting from the sidelines. Most of the time, I didn't even want to show my face around campus, I was so hurt. Adjusting to not playing was hard accepting. In my mind, I thought I could, but physically, I wasn't fully equipped. Motivational books were getting handed to me to uplift my spirits, rehabbing and physical therapy gave me a better outlook on bouncing back, not just on the field but even spiritually. My confidence was shot, it was like I lost a superpower. I went from this big-time dude to some puny mawg walking around campus. I swear I could read minds, you see, back then I didn't know what I know now, but energy-wise, some people were happy I was injured. I swear there were some teehee's and some haha's going on telepathy-wise. Good thing I'm not a weak person.

I was destined to bounce back. Furthermore, I was eager to become disciplined enough to grasp and strive once and for all at this college education that I thought was design for me to fail. Well, I was unconscious that it was designed to make you fail later in life by being systematically programmed to live under one's command, facts. Over 50% of the people with degree never manage to book a gig in what they graduated with. Since Kindergarten, it has been a setup. Luckily in my life, the way it's set up, it's like, me being from the suburbs and the city. I got street smarts and school smarts, taking the discipline ways of school, and applying them to entrepreneurship. Some feel a college education is a waste of time and money to go to school graduate and can't get a job in the field in which they obtain their degree. In the year 2021, it's not a thing of going to college graduating following the traditional ways of society. The ways of society now, on the go, it's the hustle, and bustle. Don't get me wrong, it is people who found success in their college education. I think the judging comes in when it pertains to, "Are you your own boss?" Did you get sucked into the matrix, where it's no breaking it because you are going with the flow and not being the flow? Get the drift.

To even obtain a degree, shit starts with going with the flow. So that's just what I started doing. I had no idea how many beautiful women would be at the library or computer lab. The first time I step inside the library, it was foreign to me. Seeing students that you see in a regular setting that you had no idea they took their schooling as seriously as they did were faithfully in the library. I think I felt like the only one to not belong in the library, I thought I was too cool for that shit, being smart, it was corny to be smart where I grew up from. And if you were smart or a nerd, the ones that were considered cool often picked and preyed on the nerd's weakness. I never got a kick out of messing with someone who never had the urge to be in the crowd. A lot of my homies and I got a kick out of whooping the toughest person's ass or treating them like some goofy. You have some real and thorough people that wouldn't dare allow you to pick on someone that's not with the shits. This was a period of transformation, transforming into being this big-time jock as they call it, into a humbling student, striving to graduate on time. This was the true turning point for me consciously. I realize that it was cool to be smart. I had cut back on participating in any footballs curricular activities because I was focused on rehabbing and getting back to a 100%. At the time, internally, I thought I only had two decisions to make once my knee injury occurred. Those two options were, heading back to the block and entering back in the world and getting some money, or adjust to bettering my IQ level; so when I do get out here in the world, I could run my own block and make great decisions pertains to getting some money, all because I smarten up. Own something.

CHAPTER 26

UNIVERSITY ENLIGHTENMENT

Impressive being from where I was from, going through what I went through, and carrying myself the way I carried myself while walking the campus. Stereotypically speaking, man, some real-life thugs enrolled in college seeking a better life and going to the library way before me. It's weird seeing guys from the block, buck 150's and Pelle Pelle's on, with the image of a D-Boy, but he was enrolled in college, yea, some locals. Fascinating, it made me feel comfortable even trying to be educated or intellectual. Suppose it wasn't for the prep talk with my mom about even giving this education thing a shot after my knee injury. I straight up told my mother when I got hurt, I wasn't there for no school, I was there for football, football that's it, that all. For any of my athletes reading this book, I'm not trying to strike nerve but think about the point in time when you got injured any time of your career, and you battled with throwing in the towel, not attack the situation, bouncing back cause you a warrior. Nothing against those that could have overcome that adversity, but confidence-wise, no longer resided in them. Some injuries you can't come back from, a small percentage of ballplayers tear their ACL and still get drafted or playing in the professional sports league. A special breed overcomes this injury and restore the confidence to trust you can compete at the high level, its different type of focus.

My focus was staying balance at this time, I had too much low frequency vibes, I was trying not to adjust to, between the injury, feeling illiterate, throwing in the towel, and being looked at as a college student, it was all type of shit going on in my head. They have the nerve to look at Marijuana as a bad thing. Shit'n me. Shout out to my people with an illness that gets prescribed some good weed to overcome whatever pain they endure. They hate on the weed, but I accomplish so much being on cloud 9. If they had hidden some money in a book at this time, I might have found every dollar because I became one reading guy. At first, I couldn't comprehend what I was being shown at this given moment. As I mentioned before, football was not forever, and a light bulb clicked in my head, let me get this education. They say it takes about 21 days for a habit, by the 30th day of consistently habitually going to the library, meeting with tutors, I began to sharpen my student iron. The only thing I was not trying to get used to, were some damn crutches assisting me with the limp that had me vulnerable. The crutches would have turn into some drill team batons, but I was already defeated if my ops wanted to demonstrate in any type of festivities. Once I realized, everyone was there to get a degree despite being a top athlete, or if you thought you were going to the league, I started to think more from an intellectual standpoint. The injury just showed me how fast things could change, so at this point, I began to seize the moment.

I smartened up on their ass. Coaches seen a change instantly, I know what they were thinking, I drop out, give up, someone else could use my scholarship. Emotions bottled up, confused, raged, angry, sad, defeated, humiliated, everything you could think of on the low-frequency plane to alter one neuron, had my nerves all screwed up. My Angelic beings, guiding me through these obstacles that were set before me, bless me with the strength to fight the fight, it's no other option but to stick it out, even though it was easier to just skip it. It was harder to dig deep inside and find the GOD within me and fight my battle on a spiritual level.

Slowly but surely, day by day, I was strengthening my aura back to more vibrant color. I still rocked my all-black attire regularly; it was more of a protection talisman. More protection from the dark thoughts projected onto me to get tricked out of my spot. I wasn't going. Now I was competing with myself, something I had done subliminally along my journey. I always managed to push myself to great heights, and that was charging back up my superpowers and become what I had my mindset to be. The league wasn't looking so promising as it was when I was fully charged up. With your own eyes, you saw my Merkabah reached the maximum radius it could beam. No matter the circumstances, it continued to rotate, I was back and forth, with my day usually beginning at 6:30 am with rehab. My 8:30 class elaborated on my future without football. Communication is one of the more important things that control society. Visual and Audio communications are arts in art if that sounds right. My late-night radio show from 10-12 pm was still booming as I found somewhat of a way to express myself and be heard. I filled my void going to the radio station to talk on the air about random subjects.

Here and there, I would give my input on the season and what could be done to win. Most of the time, the show was impromptu, but our platform was structured with some professional drops, we held a top spot-on college radio at a point in time. Every class during that semester I was enrolled in consisted of developing my communication skills. I got introduced to Tv and film. Editing on avid pro was my goal once I mastered Adobe Premiere. Public speaking, I had to sharpen up my on- camera appearance.

Just l as it was people that probably want to see me fail, it was also those that rooted to see me come back even stronger. With my injury recovery at about 70 percent, only about 10 percent of my confidence had needed to be restored. During this whole adversary, I bent but never folded. In my little world, I was just doing me. I was symbolically this big-time jock, but in my mind, I knew every single being walking that campus didn't know who I was. That always kept me grounded and humble. If that's not the case, it's many people that don't follow sports. I was beginning to focus more on being a productive student because I realized football wasn't forever. Being regular, attending class, focusing more on more books, I stop feeling so dumb of myself when trying to comprehend basic assignments worth big points.

The 10-page paper isn't due to two class sessions out, I was knocking out the same day it was given. Academically, I was starting to function like a regular student. I never flexed my muscle or at least took advantage of some of my perks and incentives as an athlete. The reason being is that I never had the luxury of getting comfortable with having a consistent football year. Later in my college life, for a while had me feeling like being a student-athlete was all a setup for failure in a realistic world. That same big-time athlete that must suffer from injury, longevity scars, or emotional rollercoaster, and spells cast on to them for a scholarship or million-dollar contracts, grind and works hard for every dollar, even credit hour. It just isn't no walk in the park.

It took until life after college for me to grasp the fact that it's a person just as rich as our well-known athlete in the world, and all he does is wake up in the AM and presses a button. Hypothetically speaking, stock options. Many have clocked in at 9:30 am and made a massive amount of income. At 9:45 am, they might have made one's salary in one woo wop. Never leaving home, access to freedom, and director of their own movie. Athlete or not, who wants to shed blood, sweat, and tears for a currency with no power. I rather twiddle my toes, eat a big ass bowl of cereal after I wake and bake, sit back, press a couple of buttons in the stock market and chill out. Work smart and not hard.

Honestly, I had worked so hard to be eligible my first year, struggling with grasping the college lifestyle. I wanted to throw the towel in multiple times. That's right, although I just explained how hard I worked up until that point and going through what I went through to build my character. Not saying I didn't want to do right, it's just the nature of where I'm from, to just go with the flow, rather right or wrong. Especially in this instance, to me, it was balanced. I was the man on the field now, Fake Famous, off the field I still maintain the gangster persona. Being on RaRa, was a part of me. It took something crucial to happen to me for me to want to do right, internally. I was forced to do shadow work without me knowing the meaning of the term.

I still had dark thoughts about the guy that injured me during the Wake Forest game. Bitter, and sweet must I say. In all actuality, it made me look forward to the future, life in the NFL. I continued to dream of playing in the NFL not only to make history and win a couple of Championships but to get my lick back on the guy that blew my knee out. Yea, I know, was I honestly thinking like this at the time? Yes, you think I was knocking out the same guy while enrolled, you could only imagine the thoughts I had if I made it to the NFL as I stood across from my opponent. I was taking it beyond football the next time I saw him, yea I was on my Chipolar shit and wouldn't feel good until he felt my pain. That next year, he got drafted by the NY Jets. I might have a change of heart if we played on the same team, once I made it to the league, my mind was made up, probably just punched him in his mouth and stomped him out. It's an ignorant thought process to have entering the NFL, not knowing, it was a fair ballgame, between the whistles. I just felt like he had it out for me, and who knows, they were probably all working together, I just got caught slipping. A Chicago person who vibrates low until they reach that high frequency is looking to get our get back.

CHAPTER 27

VALUE OF SELF

First, I had to get my ass back on the field and back to 100 percent. The road to recovery consisted of not just the physical aspect but spirituality as well. Thank God I had some spiritual foundation and a support system to make it through that season, only playing seven plays of the first game against Wake Forest. I had never been so humble in my life before this injury. I became one of the coolest people, despite having at least one enemy who would have loved to catch me while I was vulnerable. Respectfully, I was too focused on getting caught slipping. Dedicating this time to rehab and schoolwork, it was going to be hard just catch me on one leg like everything was sweet. This transformation was much needed as I began to move differently than I did before. Yes, I did miss a step, the injury did slow me down, but it was up to me mentally to press on and finish out my football career and graduate. It just required a different type of focus.

The best thing throughout this whole ordeal is that I stayed busy, busy enough to compensate for the feeling of stardom being taking away due to the injury. Ego tripping, during this time I had discovered what I wanted to major in, and I never from day one ever thought about that. Communications Media Studies was introduced, which was conducive to sports and the entertainment industry. Remember, the radio show I was conducting was getting me just as much recognition as me playing football. This Communication degree I was enrolled in public speaking they said it would also properly prepare one to speak politically correctly, I want to say.

Fast forward to the next season, I was back active, happy to be back out there with the guys. I know what it took me to get back playing and competing with the confidence I had before. I gained that step back, but carving down my meniscus, now rubbing bone to bone, and a custom-made knee brace for protection, slowed me down a tad bit. I battled more with trying not to think about another football hit being out on me. That next one, I would be out of the game forsaken. So, I played somewhat timid but was always on point. We kicked the season off going 7-0, beating some big-time teams like Maryland and Alabama. Alabama was the biggest win by far that year and might be for school history. Huskies, 19, Crimson Tide 16, and we were playing at Alabama with over 100,000 in attendance. Can you say Lit? Super Lit. We finished the season off 10-2, with our first loss against Bowling Green University.

NIU ranked at #9, this time collectively as a team, this brought much attention to the university and the town. All of this was fine and dandy at the time, but surviving a full game became more of a survival mode for me. For anyone I have had to put these hands-on, I sincerely apologize because the knee injury alone with the psychological effects I had to deal with to remain a high-caliber ballplayer was challenging. I was ready to throw the towel in with the football shit a couple of times. Especially since I crack the code of my intellectual abilities to learn and memorize what I was learning that year being off hurt was tugging away to my other side, sometimes I had too much time, and with that time, I liked not having to do all that football festivities. At this point, if they were going to take me out, they were going to take me out, or I was going to let them take me out. Me letting them take me out wasn't an option, so every time I stepped on the field, I said a prayer, knowing I was sacrificing my body, went out there and tried to demolish any and everybody, between the whistles.

Why did they let me get back right and see through the illusion of fear? I ended up forgetting about my knee and stop acting like a little bitch. See the thing in this football world; it's like gladiators, gladiating. I'm referring to a fight where the fighters are slugging it out and let the best man win type, gladiators. The moment you keep getting hoo-hah hit, meaning another football player hitting you like a rag doll, the more football life gets snatched from you. I learned that early on.

I don't get hit; I do the hitting. I think I explained that early in the book. Applying this trait learn from Dolton Bears Oklahoma drill playing widget ball, I tapped into myself to continue playing on this bum knee. They say GOD is inside you for the chosen ones, I unconsciously knew I was a GOD cause all I had was me to believe in. What's that saying, I search for myself and found GOD, and I found GOD, I found myself. You battle with so many things along the way of righteousness. Nobody's perfect, but what're your intentions? I didn't intend ever to change, and when I speak in that aspect! I'm talking in the part of being a so call Real Nigga, or a Real GOD from the Southside of Chicago, that worked hard so get a scholarship and still maintain his gangsterism. The most dangerous part about gangsterism is that it was starting to be more prestigious, and that came from me being studious of my surroundings. That loudest one in the room is usually the weakest in the room, I didn't have to say much, with me back balling on the field, radio show popping, off the field that dude, anything else, I would be doing too much. I always felt like this, so I just always tried to be super cool. Being focus is the key. Lack of focus once again can deter one from obtaining their set goal.

Character is something I never got into; I was just doing me—too many actors. Anything I did was not out of character; all I knew was to be myself. I was so wrapped up in doing the right thing that I looked up and was on track to graduate. It seems like yesterday I was just struggling to complete a four-page paper, and in December, I would walk the stage. Who would have ever thunk it? As dumb as I had felt, something stuck with me that I will never forget an upperclassman shared with me. He said, "C's and D's, get degrees. Lifetime hack for someone that's thinking about going to college but struggles in getting good grades. I'm not encouraging you to go party your college life away and do the bare minimum, but the grades are going to average out, as long as you don't get any F's. Although you might be looking to major in Computer Science, you could cut a couple of corners and switch your degree to General Studies, and wala, you'll be graduating in four years. Going through this process did it for me, withstanding every storm that came which way. The days that it did rain, I knew deep in my soul that the Sun would eventually shine. I know the Sun is a million miles away, and I am a reflection of it. Although I often had dark thoughts in my mind during some football games, always felt like I was going to get hurt again, I think about what I'm writing right now, where I'm from, we were born to live in survival mode, cause that mode kicked in, just like any other time I had to figure out what threw my energy out of whack.

I survived that season. Some would say I balled out; I would say I did all right. I had well over a hundred tackles, a couple of interceptions, and racked up some kick- off return yards. What would it be like if I never got hurt? I might just tap into the Akashic records and see if it's even in the records. I was just thinking from a metaphysic aspect. So, the thing with graduating! I walked the stage that Month of May.

I had treated graduation like it wasn't an accomplishment after working so hard to get on course to get to that day. My mom and I had different outlooks, and I get it a mother wants to see her son receive a diploma, especially college. For some reason, when I got to that point, it was nothing to me. My eighth-grade graduation was right across the street from my house on Thornridge football field, I walked there. Robeson High School started with 400 freshmen, I was 1 out of 43 to walk the stage, which the set up was dead smack in the middle of the parking lot by the tennis court. I was looking at my college graduation, like a party I wasn't trying to attend. A baby blue Girbaud sweater with the brown strap going across the front of it, with the blue Girbauds, brown straps, if you remember them jeans, that style. And I had on some damn brown and light blue Fila's on, high top with the strap. I just didn't feel like putting on a suit and tie. It was a big accomplishment at the time, But I had failed my math 101 class, which was my second time taking that math class— one of the most maximum illusions that took place in my life. I graduated, walked the stage, and received a blank diploma. That diploma wouldn't be filled in until I passed that math 101 class.

CHAPTER 28

SENIOR SEASON

Heading into my last football season, I made it all about football, football, and football only. Visualizing the life of an NFL player, my senior year, I was bringing it into fruition. I lined things up, but truly wasn't nothing in order. My math class should have been my first priory. It always plays in my mind of a quote I heard from a coach when I first step on the football field. He made a joke but was dead as serious. He emphasized that the school was first, holding up two fingers, and proceeding to say football second, holding up the first finger. What did I do? Put football first. I was just chilling, felt like I had made it, and didn't make shit, but the second-team all-conference team. It was my last go-around; I had got granted the previous season because I received a medical redshirt. Man, not attending that class, I had too much time on my hands. Already indulging on the radio scene, I was getting acquainted with the music scene. The first time getting introduced to making beats was my freshman year, Grant North. I was intrigued by how the young producer pieced loops together to create a melodic tune with a soulful feeling. He was cold, he might of went on and did something with the music, I just forget his name. But by my senior year, with so much time on my hand, a couple of me and the homies started a rap group called street team. Now, mind you, this is like 2003, 2004. Right around the same time, Kanye West dropped college dropout. Fast forward the knowledge in 2021 about the effect music plays on one's life. In that small window, I was willing to say fuck football after hearing that album. You couldn't tell me that wasn't my calling when I got intune to make beats and rapping. I have always been a dope writer, but some of the closest homies use to say I was trash.

Hating, I bout could have blown up, the way the game is now. Offbeat, unorthodox cadence, untraditional flows is what we in the hip-hop society have got dumb down too. Whole different type of vibe, then the 80's, 90's, and the early 2000's. Mastering something comes from much practice, like how I mastered being an athlete in my sports days. Not knowing I was a genius at the time, it was hard for me to kick a dope flow on the beat, but I could make a song. The more and more I recorded a song, then I felt I could become a rapper. I could probably go in the lab now and bang a song out and be on beat because I have been a student of the game for a while. Respectfully saying this, rapping is not for everyone.

I knew it wasn't for me, and I had football dreams about playing on Sundays. The big league is where I belonged. I felt it, and I knew if I just buckled down this last season, I would get a shot. So, entering that season with a chip on my shoulder, I embraced the egotistical side of my insecurity of not feeling like the football player I once did before the injury. Now a graduate, trying to rap, hustling a little bit to hustle, and a whole different total outlook of honestly playing in the NFL. Playing football, sadly but true, is something until later on in life I felt like I was only good at. I mean, I knew I was an elite in other sports, but I was talking beyond sports.

What was my God-given talent, what am I here to do? I never once thought about that until I hit that brick wall. The brick wall eventually came tumbling down, but I either knocked it down, or I'm a superhero and have superpowers, vibrate at a high frequency, and walked through the wall. Cause when I look back, the wall still up and some people trying to get over it, or run through it, and here I am with an activated Merkabah and be flying through shit—speaking presently about self. I think it's just the leadership in me.

During the summer leading up to my last season, I was nominated as team Co- Captain. It was an honor to become one of the captains of the team. My whole goal was always to lead a team to a Championship, having won one since my first year playing with the Dolton Bears. We had turned the NIU program around the last three seasons, ranking in the top 25 a couple of times. So, the expectations of my senior year were high, except for me.

I had fallen back off the smoke after getting pulled into the office and informed of a random drug test. This was discussed among the captains, and I didn't want to raise any alarms of me smoking weed. I did some miraculous thing on the field when I smoked. Now, I never got high before any game, fuck no, I had enough self- discipline not to do that cause when I use to be hooping high, everything moved in slow motion. So, I couldn't chance that. But it was part of my daily regimen. It was time to fall back though, just didn't want to get caught and piss dirty. I remember my freshman year, I wasn't even active, never stepped a foot in the stadium or workout facilities. Receiving a call one day out of the blue to come to take a piss test, they caught me in a frenzy. Walgreens right up the street, I grabbed a bottle of Niacin, and itched and scratched, for about twenty minutes drunk and bunch of water, went in there and pissed. I raised a red flag cause I drunk too much water, the lady asked me why my piss was diluted, I told her that I loved H2O. I guess I passed. When I wasn't smoking, it's like I lost my magic, I was now entering into their matrix. I started stinking the field up, all because I wasn't smoking, it's like I lost my imagination to get an interception and take it to the house. I felt robotic, I felt weak as hell, that's how I felt. I made plays, but I didn't see myself standing out. When I say, I felt weak, meaning I was just out there playing, and my worst game might have been one of your favorite football player's best games. By Mid-season, I was taking the risk and fired up the first blunt so I could tap in. After taking two losses at the beginning of the season, we went on a winning spree before facing our rivalry, Toledo. I had already snagged up four interceptions, and this fasho was going to be a passing game. Their quarterback threw for 300 hundred yards, getting most of those yards off a simple wide receiver screen, and when they did, decide to go long. Five wide, empty backfield, DB pinpoint their wide receivers, damn TE slipped out, one missed tackle, and they scored, I swear that wasn't my man, might have been though. All I know is whoever betted on us, lost some money, and was bout mad at me because I missed the tackle, shit happens.

Unfortunately, once again, we were beaten by Toledo University, during my last season. We were never able to beat them. After that loss, we went on to go on the rest of the season and finish 8-3, 7-1 in the conference. Before that, we went 10-2 and didn't even get a nomination for a bowl game. Then, we were invited to play in the Silicon Valley Football classic game against Troy University. It was the first time being in a bowl since 1983, we were making history 20 years later. I had a lot to be excited for, but once again, the false enthusiasm we were supposed to play before Troy, you can't tell me it isn't a conspiracy theory. I forget whom we were supposed to play, but where we were supposed to play is what had me turned up to the max—scheduled to play in Shreveport, Louisiana. They say there are no coincidences. Shreveport, Louisiana is where Dad is from, my family there, do you understand that the energy I was going to be able to feed off of being where I had roots deeply embedded in that soil of that stadium. I would have had the whole Shreveport there, I was going to go crazy, like Chipolar crazy. I was going to tap so far into my Chi, aligned up my pole where I would be able to be one with the universe and shine so bright like a star. I saw it, I dreamed it, a couple of days later, they moved our game to San Jose, California. Playing in Shreveport, Louisiana, the last game of my collegiate career, would have been too electrifying for one player to have all that power. Before I knew what the Akashic records were, I tapped into them during meditation a couple of days after hearing we were playing in Louisiana, and I saw vividly, what I was going to do in that game was going to boost my NFL stock so high, I was going to break the algorithm of the draft.

CHAPTER 29

TAPPING IN

I kept that same energy when I heard we were going to play In the Silicon Valley football classic. I kept my focus, the first was to win that bowl, and the second was to get Defensive MVP. I was all the way locked in on those two, wasn't anything else to focus on at the time. Although San Jose and San Fransisco is a beautiful place, it was just something about the energy there or the itinerary they had set up for us. Shit was a distraction. Soon as we land and arrive at the hotel, given a stipend of a couple of hundred dollars to kick it and buy what you wanted. I came back home with every dollar. They could have paid us every game in that case, from how I see it. Man, in them bowl games, they lay it out for the college teams and players. We are talking about both the Silicon Valley Football classic, not the Rose Bowl, I could just imagine how their itinerary and the stipend for playing in one of those big-time bowls. The whole energy play on that for the players goes like this, this is just my theological perspective. At that time, the ones that for sure going pro, it's the portal to walk thru, that dimension you enter, which is the vast spectrum of the NFL life. Another portal is where that game and that game is a dimension for those who will only reach that height in their football career like it's over with after this game. This about as close it will get to a professional feeling pertaining to football. Then you have the portal of the one where this dimension is where one gets stuck in the higher realm and might slip up and stay at that high frequency, this bowl game gives him an extra boost to vibrate high enough to get picked up a free agent or whatever is associated with going to play unexpectedly professionally. Whichever dimension you get sucked in at that time, if you are not all the way Intune at that given void, sometimes it is just to seize the moment.

I was living in the moment while everyone was out enjoying the little hundreds, they have given us, I spent much of the time in my hotel room, envisioning us winning this bowl game. Selfishly speaking, I also imagined myself winning the MVP of the game. They did any and everything to play on my energy, first game rescheduled was suppose to be played in Shreveport Louisiana, they knew the cables were on me, and I was charging all the way up, but they tried to throw every wrench in the game, for one, it rained like a motherfucker, and stormed. It probably was an artificial storm. I had to conserve so much of my energy through my thoughts and meditation, I felt electrifying. They blamed it on the storm, but we had electrical transformer malfunctioning, so they say which cause a blackout for the beginning of the first quarter. They felt the energy, we were all turned up, and wasn't any turning us down. Pouring down cats and dogs didn't stop both teams from making it a passing game. It reminded me of playing in my widget football game. New Lennox vs. Dolton Bears, where it rained heavily, and the ground was covered with mud, and it was the mud bowl. We went back and forth, scoring in the first quarter, putting up 14 points apiece. Troy wasn't no punks, this is the year they had a great Defensive end, an excellent running back they had, but nothing like ours at the time, G-Wolfe. Every time he touched the ball, G was taking it to the house. This game had to be balanced out due to the rain altering plans for both teams. Pass, run, was our game plan, the more they pass the ball, would be gambling to their offense at a critical time. Booyah, they were definitely gambling throwing my way, with the assistance of the rain, and already a fire sign, I worked some magic and got me an interception, returning it for about 15 yards. That made my five interceptions of the season. Throughout the game, I made some key plays recording ten tackles. I didn't feel like I balled out, it was many obstacles to face that game. The most important thing is that we won. Won a bowl game for the first time in school history since 1983. With the power of meditation, I tapped in and received the 2004 defensive MVP of the bowl.

Tapping in from here on out was mandatory. I knew the power of the mind, but not the power of the mind as I know now. What I know now is that I can manifest anything I put my mind to. I was testing a superpower that would be needed later on in life. That's why it's that saying, "a mind is a terrible thing to waste." So, me envisioning me receiving MVP shows the power of the mind. Us winning the Bowl Championship shows the power of the mind when we're all on one accord. Collectively it was a great look for our program. Twenty-something years is a long time for anything to experience a feeling you once experience that made you feel like you were on top of the world. I was only 22 years old; I was experiencing that feeling in increments, long as intervals somewhat. For example, when I enrolled back in high school or became eligible to play college football and receive a scholarship. It is not so much of my accomplishments, but more of the self- discipline, self-love, and self-care strengthening I received to endure my life path struggles beyond football. After celebrating the achievement of being bowl champs, the feeling of loneliness would begin to trigger. This wasn't the feeling I had wanted during my isolation meditation tactic to get the MVP or the energy I put in to see us win as bad as the fans or coaches who had invested so much into this feeling for the last umpteen years. It was almost equivalent to the sense of when I blew my knee out. I was forced to tap into my inner chi. Being from the chi, your inner chi is a different type of force to conquer. Conquering that means you are one with yourself. My next journey required some isolation, the season was over, and now this tiny window was opening for me to finally live out my childhood dream. Well, wasn't never my childhood dream, it was more of something I thought I had to do or was going to do. In the football world, the amount of time and energy I put into mastering the characteristic of an NFL type of player was massive. From 7 years old, now 22, I had built my opportunity to be playing Sundays. Like most seniors who went through the 4-year process and getting his letters, if that athlete was on the radar of any scout, rather them going to the combine or private workout with NFL teams, he might just have a shot.

As can be seen, I was heavenly Invested in, since day 1, and I say that because I stuck with it. I never gave up, from becoming eligible, to the knee injury. Embedded in my spirit, I was a future NFL star since my high school coach had given me the opportunity to fill out the NFL prospect form. Would that form be the reason I live out my dream, or would it require me tapping into my Chi, aligning my mind, body, and soul, becoming one with the Universe and be

Chipolar, to be continued

AUTHOR

Lionel Hickenbottom, CEO/President of El Antron LLC. Hickenbottom originated from Dolton/Chicago, Illinois, as a well-known All-Star athlete at Paul Robeson High School on the Southside of Chicago's Englewood neighborhood; later went to further his education at NIU. (Northern Illinois University) He received his Undergraduate Degree in Communication of Media Studies in 2004. In 2005, he worked on various Film Industry projects as an extra, stand-in, and stunt double and inspiring filmmaker. He began filming independent projects as a Director, Cinematographer, Producer, and Video Editor. Furthermore, Hickenbottom's knowledge throughout his college career in Media Studies allowed him to become an Elite All-Star filmmaker specializing in Directing, Producing, Video Editing, and Operating Drones. It has earned him multiple IMDB credits in the Film Industry. Writing my first books has allowed me to add an extra edition to my expertise. During, my journey I was often blinded by the illusion to not live in my higher purpose and staying on the right path. Like many of us coming from similar places with obstacles to create struggles, becoming righteous is our nature. Coming in tune with myself and tapping into my Chi has allowed me to break down some barriers. It's my first book and one of many Love

"You must go within, in order to discover what you are looking for, what you are searching for is your higher self."

El Antron~

Want to know more?
Write to us at elantron@elantron.org

Discover great books, exclusive offers and more at
www.elantron.org

Connect with us on social media

@El Antron

@1elantron

@antron_el

CPSIA information can be obtained
at www.ICGtesting.com
Printed in the USA
LVHW110409020921
696501LV00001B/6